P9-BVG-952

Twayne's English Authors Series

Sylvia E. Bowman, *Editor*

INDIANA UNIVERSITY

Lewis Carroll

TEAS 212

Lewis Carroll

LEWIS CARROLL

By RICHARD KELLY

University of Tennessee

TWAYNE PUBLISHERS

A DIVISION OF G. K. HALL & CO., BOSTON

Library of Congress Cataloging in Publication Data

Kelly, Richard Michael, 1937–
   Lewis Carroll.

   (Twayne's English authors series; TEAS 212)
   Bibliography: pp. 155–58
   Includes index.
   1. Dodgson, Charles Lutwidge, 1832–1898—Criticism and
interpretation.
PR4612.K38   828'.8'09   77–24721
ISBN 0–8057–6681–2

Contents

About the Author

The author holds the B.A. from the City College of New York and the M.A. and Ph.D. from Duke University. His specialty is Victorian humor and poetry. He has written *Douglas Jerrold* (Twayne) and edited *The Best of Mr. Punch: the Humorous Writings of Douglas Jerrold*. He has also published articles on Lord Chesterfield, Samuel Johnson, Robert Browning, and Bulwer-Lytton. From 1970 to 1976 he was editor of *Tennessee Studies in Literature*, an annual journal of literary scholarship published by the University of Tennessee.

Since 1965 he has been a member of the English Faculty at the University of Tennessee, where he is now Professor of English. He has recently completed an edition of the great cartoonists of nineteenth-century *Punch* for Dover Publications.

Preface

The number of books and articles that have been written about Lewis Carroll is enormous, and doubtless that number will continue to grow in the future. The devoted student of Carroll finds himself in the quandary of Alice in that he has to read faster and faster just to stand still. The philosophers have analyzed Carroll's ideas, the linguists his sentences, the social critics his environment, and the psychoanalysts his mind. Yet both the man and his writings remain enigmas, still to be probed and elucidated. Despite the large number of recent studies there has not appeared in over twenty years a single book that offers a broad critical survey of Carroll's life and writings. The present volume, it is hoped, will fill this gap and suggest the many specialists to whom one might go for more detailed consideration of specific aspects of his works.

The principal aim of this book is to demonstrate Lewis Carroll's mastery of the art of nonsense, a genre which his works practically define. In order to achieve this objective I have focused my analysis and critical evaluation upon Carroll's poetry, the Alice books, and the two volumes of *Sylvie and Bruno*. Since Carroll's life has been a traditional part of discussions of his work, I have attempted to record those aspects of his biography that appeared to have the strongest bearing upon his writings. The chapter on his photography, mathematics, and miscellaneous essays is included to demonstrate how his emotional and literary interests carry over into both the practical and abstract sciences. This study does not attempt to cover in detail Carroll's puzzles, games, and serious mathematics and logic since those areas are only tangentially related to his literary productions.

Rather than advancing a narrow thesis about Carroll's major publications, this study incorporates a variety of distinguished and provocative criticism from the past and present and analyzes

Carroll's writings in the light of an informed critical heritage. A number of Carroll's works, however, such as the early nonsense, the poetry, *Sylvie and Bruno*, *Sylvie and Bruno Concluded*, and the miscellaneous essays have received little or no critical attention; and the several chapters on these lesser known works thus break new ground as they examine the merits of the pieces themselves and the critical perspective and context they provide for reading the Alice books.

For helping me in my study, I would like to thank the University of Tennessee Graduate School for a summer grant. I am especially indebted to Derek Hudson's *Lewis Carroll* for much of the information contained in Chapter One. Finally, I would like to thank my wife Barbara for her help in copyediting the manuscript.

RICHARD M. KELLY

Knoxville, Tennessee

Chronology

Thackeray, Alfred Tennyson; photographs the Tennyson family; receives his Master of Arts.

1860   Publishes *A Syllabus of Plane Algebraical Geometry* and *Rules for Court Circular*.

1861   Ordained Deacon on December 22.

1862   On July 4, makes a boating excursion up the Isis to Godstow in the company of Robinson Duckworth and the three Liddell sisters to whom he tells the story of Alice; begins writing and revising *Alice's Adventures under Ground*.

1863   Completes *Alice's Adventures under Ground* in February.

1864   In April John Tenniel agrees to illustrate Alice; on June 10, Carroll settles upon the title *Alice's Adventures in Wonderland*; on November 26, sends the manuscript of *Alice's Adventures under Ground* to Alice Liddell.

1865   Sends presentation copy of *Alice's Adventures in Wonderland* to Alice Liddell on July 4; *Alice's Adventures in Wonderland* first published in July, withdrawn in August and sent to America; the book's true second edition published in England in November by Richard Clay (erroneously dated 1866).

1866   Appleton of New York publishes the second (American) issue of the first edition of *Alice's Adventures in Wonderland*.

1867   Writes "Bruno's Revenge" for *Aunt Judy's Magazine*; tours the Continent and visits Russia with Dr. H. P. Liddon.

1868   Death of his father on June 21; in October moves into rooms in Tom Quad, Oxford, where he lives for the rest of his life.

1869   Publishes *Phantasmagoria* (verse) in January.

1871   Completes *Through the Looking-Glass and What Alice Found There* in January; the volume published in December (though dated 1872).

1875   "Some Popular Fallacies about Vivisection" published in the *Fortnightly Review*.

1876   Publishes *The Hunting of the Snark*, illustrated by Henry Holiday.

1879   Publishes *Euclid and his Modern Rivals*.

1881   Resigns from his mathematical lectureship.

Chronology

1882   Elected Curator of the Senior Common Room on December 8.

1883   Publishes a collection of his verse, *Rhyme? and Reason?*

1885   Publishes *A Tangled Tale*, a series of mathematical problems in the form of short stories originally printed in the *Monthly Packet*.

1886   Macmillan publishes the facsimile edition of Carroll's original illustrated manuscript of *Alice's Adventures under Ground*. Theatrical production of *Alice in Wonderland*.

1887   Publishes *The Game of Logic*.

1888   Publishes *Curiosa Mathematica, Part I*, a highly technical analysis of Euclid's 12th Axiom.

1889   Publishes *Sylvie and Bruno* and *The Nursery Alice*.

1893   Publishes *Sylvie and Bruno Concluded* and *Curiosa Mathematica, Part II*.

1896   *Symbolic Logic*, the last book of Carroll's to appear in his lifetime.

1898   Dies on January 14 at his sisters' home at Guildford; *Three Sunsets and Other Poems* published posthumously.

CHAPTER 1

Life and Time

I *Family and School*

L EWIS Carroll was born on January 27, 1832, in the parsonage
of Daresbury, Cheshire. The third child and the eldest son
of the eleven children of the Reverend Charles Dodgson and
Frances Jane Lutwidge, he was descended from two North
country families with a long tradition of service to the Church
and to the State. During his sixteen years at Daresbury the Rev.
Charles Dodgson established a Sunday school, arranged lectures,
and served the poor of the parish. In addition to his strenuous
duties as a clergyman, he published a translation of Tertullian
and wrote several books on theological and religious subjects.
His austere, puritanical, and authoritarian personality apparently
helped to mold the public character of his son who was later
to become a quiet, reserved mathematician. Mrs. Dodgson, on
the other hand, has been described as "one of the sweetest and
gentlest women that ever lived, whom to know was to love. The
earnestness of her simple faith and love show forth in all she
did and said; she seemed to live always in the conscious presence
of God."[1] Although this sketch of her is obviously exaggerated,
the love and affection that Carroll felt towards his mother was
exceptional. It has even been suggested that because of the
all-embracing love of his mother Carroll was never to displace
or develop his feelings for her to include that of another grown
woman and thus never, it seems, to have gained reasonable
confidence in himself as a man.[2]

Carroll's self-confidence may also have been hampered by his
habit of stammering, a childhood affliction that persisted throughout his life. It is possible, but unproven, that this disability may
have been caused by attempts to correct Carroll's left-handedness,
a condition, Florence Becker Lennon observes, that "may have

produced a feeling that something about him was not 'right.' "³
Throughout his life Carroll was fascinated by peculiar symmetries
and odd reversals, including mirror-writing, looking-glass worlds,
and the spelling of words backwards (Bruno, in *Sylvie and
Bruno*, exclaims that "evil" spells "live" backwards). In 1856
he had written the following lines, which later became part of
"Upon the Lonely Moor": "And now if e'er by chance I put /
My fingers into glue / Or madly squeeze a right-hand foot /
Into a left-hand shoe."⁴ The White Knight, who sings this song,
is the prototype of the left-handed man in a right-handed
world. "If Charles was reversed," Lennon argues, "he took his
revenge by doing a little reversing himself."⁵

Little is known about the years Carroll spent at the parsonage
in Daresbury. In a poem written in 1860, however, there is
evidence that Carroll recalled those early years with great
pleasure: "An island farm, mid seas of corn / Swayed by the
wandering breath of morn— / The happy spot where I was
born."⁶ In any event, after having lived in that secluded pastoral
town for eleven years, Carroll was removed to the rectory of
Croft, just inside the Yorkshire boundary, where his father
proudly assumed his new duties as Rector, a position awarded
him by Sir Robert Peel.

At this time Lewis Carroll was very fond of inventing games
for the amusement of his brothers and sisters. He constructed a
crude train out of a wheelbarrow, a barrel, and a small truck,
and arranged "stations" at intervals along the path in the rectory
garden. Some of Carroll's rules for the railway indicate the boy's
rich imagination:

Rules I. All passengers when upset are requested to lie still until
picked up—as it is requisite that at least 3 trains should go
over them, to entitle them to the attention of the doctor and
assistants.

II. If a passenger comes up to a station after the train has
passed the next (i.e. when it is about 100 m. off) he may not
run after it but must wait for the next.

III. When a passenger has no money and still wants to go by
the train, he must stop at whatever station he happens to be
at, and earn money—by making tea for the station master (who

drinks it all hours of the day and night) and grinding sand
for the company (what use they make of it they are not bound
to explain?).[7]

Carroll's life-long delight in number and logic and his interest
in meticulous and well-ordered detail are here in clear evidence.
Later he was to devise for the King in *Alice's Adventures in
Wonderland* "Rule Forty-two. *All persons more than a mile
high to leave the court.*"

While at Croft Carroll also amused his family by putting on
home theatricals. With the help of a village carpenter he made
a troupe of marionettes and a theater for them to perform in.
Carroll wrote most of the plays himself, the most popular being
The Tragedy of King John and La Guida di Bragia. A burlesque
of Bradshaw's Railway Guide, *La Guida* is a further example
of Carroll's interest in rules and orderliness, and Bradshaw's
speech at the close of the drama looks toward the nonsense of
The Hunting of the Snark:

> I made a rule my servants were to sing:
> That rule they disobeyed, and in revenge
> I altered all the train times in my book.[8]

Carroll extended the world of play into the various magazines
the Dodgson family produced for their own entertainment. The
first of these magazines was *Useful and Instructive Poetry*, composed for Carroll's younger brother and sister. This was followed
in later years by *The Rectory Magazine, The Comet, The Rose-
bud, The Star, The Will-O'-the-Wisp, The Rectory Umbrella,*
and *Mischmasch.* Besides editing and illustrating a number of
these magazines, Carroll contributed many humorous verses
and stories. *Useful and Instructive Poetry* contains several pieces
by him that anticipate his subsequent masterpieces of nonsense:
"A Tale of a Tail," with a drawing of a very long dog's tail,
suggestive of "The Mouse's Tail," a poem about someone who,
like Humpty Dumpty, insists upon standing on a wall but who
eventually falls off, and numerous morals that sound like those
of the didactic ugly Duchess of *Alice's Adventures in Wonderland.*

At the age of twelve, Carroll began his schooling at the Richmond Grammar School, ten miles from Croft. His classmates at first delighted in playing tricks upon him, some of which are recorded in a letter to his two eldest sisters: "they first proposed to play at 'King of the Cobblers' and asked if I would be king, to which I agreed. Then they made me sit down and sat (on the ground) in a circle round me, and told me to say 'Go to work' which I did, and they immediately began kicking me and knocking me on all sides."[9] Forced to assert himself, he soon adjusted to his new environment and was able to write that "the boys play me no tricks now." Having advanced sufficiently in his Latin and mathematics, he left Richmond at the end of 1845 and entered Rugby at the start of the following year.

Carroll recorded in his diary his impressions of the years spent at Rugby: "During my stay I made I suppose some progress in learning of various kinds, but none of it was done *con amore*, and I spent an incalculable time in writing out impositions—this last I consider one of the chief faults of Rugby School. I made some friends there . . . but I cannot say that I look back upon my life at a Public School with any sensations of pleasure, or that any earthly considerations would induce me to go through my three years again."[10] Nevertheless, Carroll worked hard at his studies and won several prizes in mathematics and classics. His true joy, however, still lay at home in Croft, which must have seemed the land of lost content. After recovering from a severe attack of whooping cough he enjoyed a pleasant interlude entertaining his brothers and sisters once more with the railway games in the rectory garden. His mother recalled the moment in a letter: "At the *Railroad* games, which the darlings *all delight* in, *he tries and proves* his strength in the most persevering way."[11] And, indeed, Carroll's strength was to persevere in the ways of a child for the rest of his life.

II   Oxford

Toward the end of 1849, after nearly four years at Rugby, Carroll returned to Croft where he prepared himself for Oxford. He matriculated at Christ Church on May 23, 1850, and went into residence as a Commoner on January 24, 1851. Only two days later he received the shocking news of his mother's death and returned home for the funeral. Archdeacon Dodgson was left with his family of eleven children, the youngest of whom was only five years old. His wife's sister, Lucy Lutwidge, came to take charge of the family and remained with them for the rest of her life. Carroll's undergraduate years thus began most unhappily. Derek Hudson wrote that "if there was one lesson above others that he brought away from Croft, it was that he could never in future, so long as he lived, be without the companionship of children. They had already become a necessity of his existence."[12]

Handicapped by a lack of money and an embarrassing stammer, Carroll kept largely to himself. Although he took a mild interest in sports, he delighted more in taking long walks or making expeditions on the river. He worked conscientiously at his studies, in 1851 winning a Boulter Scholarship and in 1852 obtaining First Class Honours in Mathematics and a Second in Classical Moderations. Dr. Edward Pusey, Oxford professor of Hebrew, acknowledged his success by nominating him to a Studentship of Christ Church. In 1854 he took his "Greats" examination and was placed in only the Third Class, philosophy and history being difficult subjects for him. While preparing for the Final Mathematical School, he managed to find time to write a poem, "The Lady of the Ladle," and a story, "Wilhelm von Schmitz," which he sent to the *Whitby Gazette*. These are the first published works by Carroll to survive. Then, at the end of October, 1854, he distinguished himself by taking a First Class in the Final Mathematical School, and on December 18 of that year he took the degree of Bachelor of Arts.

Carroll began keeping a diary in 1855 which he meticulously maintained at regular intervals to the end of his life. Before returning to Oxford on January 19, 1855, he enjoyed a period of leisure which he dutifully records in his diary. He spent several days sketching, dabbling at his mathematics, and reading such books as *The Life of Benjamin Robert Hayden*, Richard Monckton Milnes's *The Life of John Keats*, and Samuel Taylor Coleridge's *Aids to Reflection*. When he returned to Christ Church from Croft he began tutoring and preparing his mathematical lectures. In February 1855 he was appointed Sub-Librarian and in May was awarded a scholarship. "This very nearly raises my income this year to independence—Courage!"[13] he wrote in his diary. The last entry in his diary for 1855 summarizes his fortunes: "I am sitting alone in my bedroom this last night of the old year, waiting for midnight. It has been the most eventful year of my life: I began it a poor bachelor student, with no definite plans or expectations; I end it a master and tutor in Christ Church, with an income of more than £300 a year, and the course of mathematical tuition marked out by God's providence for at least some years to come. Great mercies, great failings, time lost, talents misapplied—such has been the past year."[14]

Carroll's distaste for boys, which increased as he grew older, may in part be traced back to his early attempts at teaching. He found his pupils noisy and unmanageable, and in his diary for 1856 he records some of his unpleasant experiences in the classroom: "Feb: 15. School class again noisy and troublesome—I have not yet acquired the arts of keeping order. Feb: 26. Class again noisy and inattentive—it is very disheartening, and I almost think I had better give up teaching there for the present."[15]

Finally, three days later he decides to discontinue his lectures, noting that "the good done does not seem worth the time and trouble."[16] The unexpected, disorder of any kind, greatly disturbed Carroll. His childhood games with their elaborate rules, his life-long interest in mathematics, and his elaborate file and index of all his correspondence all attest to his compulsive orderliness. If he failed to regulate the behavior of the boys in his class, he was no less disturbed that same year when he witnessed one of his fellows in an epileptic fit. He wanted to help him but did not know what to do: "I felt at the moment how helpless ignorance makes one, and I shall make a point of reading some book on the subject of emergencies, a thing that I think everyone should do."[17] Three days later he ordered *Hints for Emergencies* and began a life-long interest in medicine. Once again, this incident suggests Carroll's methodical approach to life. If he could not control his class at least he could learn how to conduct himself in emergencies. Despite his compulsive-

ness and his anxieties, however, Carroll enjoyed teaching. Besides
his public lectures, he was responsible for as many as fourteen
private pupils. Teaching, after all, was the means by which
he earned his living; and if he felt that some of his class work
was a waste of time, he more than compensated for that feeling
by instructing many students and scholars during his life through
his serious writings on logic and mathematics. As a man who
considered to his dying day that life was a puzzle, Carroll always
held the art of teaching to be an essential part of his work.

Throughout the 1850's Carroll continued to read contemporary
novels and poetry. His remarks on literature are not of much
critical interest, but they do shed some light on his own tempera-
ment. Of *Wuthering Heights*, for example, he wrote that "it is
of all novels I ever read the one I should least like to be a
character in myself. All the 'dramatis personae' are so unusual
and unpleasant. . . . Heathcliff and Catherine are original and
most powerful drawn idealities: one cannot believe that such
human beings ever existed: they have far more of the fiend
in them."[18] When one recalls that Carroll worked out elaborate
mathematical puzzles before going to sleep in order to check
his sexual fantasies (or "unholy thoughts," as he called them),
it is small wonder that the violent passions of Heathcliff and
Catherine seemed fiendish and fantastic to him.

A significant day in Carroll's life was March 18, 1856, when
he purchased his first camera. Discouraged by the *Comic Times'*
rejection of his sketches, he abandoned his notion to work as
a free-lance humorous artist and turned to the new and exacting
medium of photography. Carroll's artistic and scientific talents
could thus be nicely balanced, and he greatly enjoyed mastering
the complicated and awkward paraphernalia that photography
required at that time. During the course of his life he photographed such famous contemporaries as Alfred Lord Tennyson,
Michael Faraday, the Rossettis, John Everett Millais, Holman
Hunt, and John Ruskin, as well as members of his family,
friends, and innumerable children. Helmut Gernsheim, who
studied and collected many of Carroll's photographs, has stated
that "his photographic achievements are truly astonishing: he
must not only rank as a pioneer of British amateur photography,
but I would also unhesitatingly acclaim him as the most out-

standing photographer of children in the nineteenth century."[19]

Among the most important photogenic children in Carroll's life were the Liddell sisters: Lorina, Alice, and Edith. Soon after Henry George Liddell became dean of Christ Church in 1855 Carroll befriended his children. He first met Alice on April 25, 1856, when she was approaching her fourth birthday. He and a friend had gone to the Deanery to photograph the Cathedral, and his diary for that day reads, "The three girls were in the garden most of the time, and we became excellent friends: we tried to group them in the foreground of the picture, but they were not patient sitters." Apparently Carroll was very impressed with the children, for the entry concludes, "I mark this day with a white stone,"[20] a comment which he reserved for extraordinary occasions. The attention he gave the Liddell children was soon interpreted by some people as an attempt on his part to win the good graces of their governess, Miss Prickett, and this rumor led him to write that he would "avoid taking any public notice of the children in future, unless any occasion should arise when such an interpretation is impossible."[21]

Although Carroll's family expected him to emulate his father by marrying and establishing himself as a parish priest in one of the Christ Church livings, he grew apprehensive about such a life as the date of his ordination grew nearer. He decided to take Deacon's Orders and was ordained on December 22, 1861; but despite the urging of Dean Liddell, Carroll chose not to go on to take Priest's Orders. Meanwhile, his work in mathematics was progressing; and in 1860 he published his first book, *A Syllabus of Plane Algebraical Geometry.* In the same year he published a small pamphlet entitled *Rules for Court Circular,* which set forth the rules for a new card game he had invented. At the outset of 1861 he began his Register of Correspondence, which was to include details of every letter he wrote or received from that year to 1898. The last piece of correspondence is numbered 98,721.

III   *The Birth of Alice*

Between 1856 and 1862 Carroll continued to visit the Liddell children and amused them with many stories; but the date

July 4, 1862, is special, even though Carroll recorded it straightforwardly in his diary: "... Robinson Duckworth and I made an expedition *up* the river to Godstow with the three Liddells: we had tea on the bank there, and did not reach Christ Church again till quarter past eight, when we took them on to my rooms to see my collection of microphotographs, and restored them to the Deanery just before nine. [On the opposite page Dodgson added on Feb, 1863,]: On which occasion I told them the fairy-tale of *Alice's Adventures under Ground*, which I undertook to write out for Alice, and which is now finished (as to the text) though the pictures are not yet nearly done."[22]

Twenty-five years later the diary's matter-of-fact account of that eventful day was superceded by Carroll's idyllic description: "Full many a year has slipped away, since that 'golden afternoon' that gave thee [*Alice's Adventures in Wonderland*] birth, but I can call it up as clearly as if it were yesterday—the cloudless blue above, the watery mirror below, the boat drifting idly on its way, the tinkle of the drops that fell from the oars, as they waved so sleepily to and fro, and (the one bright gleam of life in all the slumberous scene) the three eager faces, hungry for news of fairy-land, and who would not be said 'nay' to: from whose lips 'Tell us a story, please' had all the stern immutability of Fate!"[23] It is little wonder that a man whose imagination thrived on the idealized past turned to photography in order to strike out against the passing years that were to steal his many child friends from him. In 1863, one year after the famous outing up the Isis, Carroll was no longer to see Alice Liddell with any regularity. In fact, by the time that Alice was thirteen, in 1865, Carroll wrote that she "seems changed a good deal, and hardly for the better—probably going through the usual awkward stage of transition."[24] The idyllic Alice he preserved in fiction, but the real girl, entering puberty, was now lost to Carroll forever.

Carroll completed writing *Alice's Adventures under Ground* before February, 1863, but it took him until the autumn of 1864 before he finished illustrating the manuscript. Besides planning this work as his personal gift for Alice Liddell, Carroll had by this time completed a version that expanded the original from 18,000 to 53,000 words to be illustrated by John Tenniel.

Carroll's original drawings (which can be seen in the facsimile edition of 1886), although lacking the professional sureness of line that Tenniel later provided, reveal an intense, almost nightmarish world. Consistent with his earlier work for *Punch*, Tenniel eschewed Carroll's intensity in favor of his own detached, more classical forms. Carroll rejected the title *Alice's Adventures under Ground* as being "too like a lesson book about mines," and considered *Alice's Golden Hours, Alice Among the Elves, Alice's hour in Elf-land,* and *Alice's doings in Elf-land* before finally settling upon *Alice's Adventures in Wonderland.* When Macmillan, the publishers for Oxford University, began to issue the first edition of the work, Carroll was completely unhappy with the printing of the Tenniel illustrations and in August, 1865, decided to give the printing to Richard Clay. The unbound sheets of the first edition, however, were disposed of to Appleton Publishers, New York, who published them as the second issue of the first edition in 1866. The actual second edition was published in November, 1865, by Clay.

Sales of *Alice's Adventures in Wonderland* began slowly and then gradually increased. During Carroll's lifetime over 180,000 copies, in various editions, were sold in Great Britain. Reviewers were both pleased and puzzled with the strange new book. The *Pall Mall Gazette* said that "this delightful little book is a children's feast and a triumph of nonsense." The *Reader* declared it "a glorious artistic treasure." Not all reviews, however, were so complimentary. The *Illustrated Times* thought the story was "too extravagantly absurd,"[25] and the *Athenaeum* was put off with both the tale and its illustrations:

This is a dream-story; but who can, in cold blood, manufacture a dream, with all its loops and ties, and loose threads, and entanglements, and inconsistencies, and passages which lead to nothing at the end of which Sleep's most diligent pilgrim never arrives? Mr. Carroll has laboured hard to heap together strange adventures, and heterogeneous combinations; and we acknowledge the hard labour. Mr. Tenniel, again, is square and grim, and uncouth in his illustrations, howbeit clever, even sometimes to the verge of grandeur, as is the artist's habit. We fancy that any real child might be more puzzled than enchanted by this stiff, over-wrought story.[26]

Hard words—but the above review, like most reviews of that day, assumed *Alice* was simply a book for children and as such, did not satisfy an adult's expectations. The point to keep in mind about the contemporary reaction to the book is that the Victorian reader expected a children's book to be realistic, to instruct the child in religion and morals, and consequently, to prepare him for a righteous adulthood. Carroll's book not only lacked a realistic framework but openly poked fun at conventional didacticism. Later critics arrived at a different point of view. Gilbert Chesterton, for example, declared that "it is not children who ought to read the words of Lewis Carroll, they are far better employed making mud-pies."[27] And Jan B. Gordon, in "The *Alice* Books and the Metaphors of Victorian Childhood,"[28] argues that the two Alice volumes "are decadent adult literature rather than children's literature."

During the 1860's Carroll made the acquaintance of several literary and artistic figures, including the Rossettis, John Everett Millais, Holman Hunt, Arthur Hughes, Tom Taylor, and Charlotte Yonge. Carroll saw to it that many of the presentation copies of *Alice* got into the hands of such prominent and influential people. Christina Rossetti's acknowledgment reads, in part: "My Mother and sister as well as myself have made ourselves quite at home yesterday in Wonderland, and (if I am not shamefully old for such an avowal) I confess it would give me sincere pleasure to fall in with that conversational rabbit, that endearing puppy, that very sparkling dormouse. Of the Hatter's acquaintance I am not ambitious, and the March Hare may fairly remain an open question...."[29] Her brother, Dante Gabriel Rossetti, thought that "Father William" and Alice's snatches of poetry were the funniest things he had seen in a long time.[30]

Carroll continued publishing books and pamphlets on mathematical subjects, such as *Enunciations of Euclid* (1863) and *Guide to the Mathematical Student* (1864). Most of his work on mathematics, however, was not of lasting significance. Critics seem to think that his best works on the subject were those of his later years: *Euclid and his Modern Rivals* (1879) and his edition of *Euclid I and II* (1882). But now that Euclid has been largely replaced by other forms of geometry, the interest in those works derives largely from their wit and humor and not from their illumination of mathematics.

IV *Russia*

In order to escape the occasional tedium of his Mathematical Lectureship, Carroll made a few short excursions in England, Wales, and the Isle of Wight; but on the whole he preferred to stay at home. His only trip abroad came in 1867 when he and Canon Henry Parry Liddon, later Dean of St. Paul's, visited Russia. He prepared for the tour with the greatest care that he be provided for every contingency. All details of the journey were meticulously planned in advance. He even packed letters needing to be answered and the stamped envelopes in which to mail his replies. He also kept a diary during his travels; and it reveals, besides the tourist's eye for churches and art works, some very colorful sketches of human interest. When they landed at Calais he noted that the usual swarm of friendly natives greeted them with offers of services and advice: "To *all* such remarks I returned one simple answer 'non!' It was probably not strictly applicable in all cases, but it answered the purpose of getting rid of them; one by one they left me, echoing the 'Non!' in various tones, but all expressive of disgust. After Liddon had settled about the luggage, we took a stroll in the market-place, which was white with the caps of the women, full of their shrill jabbering. . . ."[31]

Carroll frequently records the play and appearance of children he came upon. In Germany he encountered a large group of children dancing around in a ring, holding hands, and singing: "Once they found a large dog lying down, and at once arranged their dance around it, and sang their song to it, facing inwards for that purpose: the dog looked thoroughly puzzled at this novel form of entertainment, but soon made up his mind that it was not to be endured, and must be escaped at all costs."[32] Two days later he saw a less pleasant sight: "On our way to the station, we came across the grandest instance of the 'Majesty of Justice' that I have ever witnessed—A little boy was being taken to the magistrate, or to prison (probably for picking a pocket?). The achievement of this fact had been entrusted to two soldiers in full uniform, who were solemnly marching, one in front of the poor little creature, and one behind; with bayonets fixed of course, to be ready to charge in case he should attempt an escape. . . ."[33]

When he at last gets to St. Petersburg it appears to him as a sort of spacious and colorful wonderland:

We had only time for a short stroll after dinner, but it was full of wonder and novelty. The enormous width of the streets (the secondary ones seem to be broader than anything in London), the little droshkies that went running about, seemingly quite indifferent as to running over anybody (we soon found it was necessary to keep a very sharp lookout, as they never shouted, however close they were upon us)—the enormous illuminated signboards over the shops, and the gigantic churches, with their domes painted blue and covered with gold stars—the bewildering jabber of the natives—all contributed to the wonders of our first walk in St. Petersburg.[34]

His description of Moscow is equally picturesque, with the ubiquitous droshky drivers adding the touch of unreality:

We gave 5 or 6 hours to a stroll through this wonderful city, a city of white and green roofs, of conical towers that rise one out of another like a foreshortened telescope; of bulging gilded domes, in which you see as in a looking glass, distorted pictures of the city; of churches which look, outside, like bunches of variegated cactus (some branches crowned with green prickly buds, others with blue, and others with red and white), and which, inside, are hung all round with Eikons and lamps, and lined with illuminated pictures up to the very roof; and finally of pavement that goes up and down like a ploughed field, and droshky-drivers who insist on being paid 30 per cent extra today, 'because it is the Empress' birthday.'[35]

After being abroad for over two months Carroll described his return to England with poetic nostalgia: "I remained on the bow most of the time of our passage, sometimes chatting with the sailor on the lookout, and sometimes watching, through the last hour of my first foreign tour, the lights of Dover, as they slowly broadened on the horizon, as if the old land were opening its arms to receive its homeward bound children."[36] Carroll never again left England and seldom mentioned his Russian tour in later life. As Hudson points out, the trip "seems not to have touched him vitally, but if anything to have deepened his patriotic insularity."[37] Florence Lennon sees him as a paradoxical traveller who was "most English when travelling, and most foreign at home."[38]

Shortly after his return from Russia in 1867 Carroll sent a short fairy tale called "Bruno's Revenge" to *Aunt Judy's Magaznie*. This story, which he later developed into a novel, *Sylvie and Bruno* (1889), greatly pleased the editor, Mrs. Gaty, who wrote, "It is beautiful and fantastic and childlike.... Some of the touches are so exquisite, one would have thought nothing short of intercourse with fairies could have put them into your head."[39] The news he received from Croft, however, provided no occasion for joy: his father had taken suddenly ill and died. "The greatest blow that has ever fallen on my life," Carroll reflected years later.[40] He spent several weeks at home settling affairs and relocating his sisters at "The Chestnuts," a Georgian house near Guildford. When he returned to Oxford he moved into new quarters in Tom Quad, where he was to reside for the rest of his life.

V Looking-Glass *and* Snark

On August 24, 1866, Carroll wrote to Macmillan's, "It will probably be some time before I again indulge in paper and print. I have, however, a floating idea of writing a sort of sequel to 'Alice,' and if it ever comes to anything, I intend to consult you at the very outset, so as to have the thing properly managed from the beginning."[41] In 1868, the idea progressed, Carroll began writing, and after considerable persuading, John Tenniel agreed to do the illustrations. Carroll incorporated many of his earlier writings into the manuscript, including "Jabberwocky" (the first stanza of which he completed in 1855), and "Upon the Lonely Moor," the parody of William Wordsworth which he published in 1856 in *The Train*.

The first inspiration for *Through the Looking-Glass* came from a conversation Carroll had with his little cousin, Alice Raikes, during August of 1868. Alice later recorded the incident:

We followed him into his house which opened, as ours did, upon the garden, into a room full of furniture with a tall mirror standing across one corner.

"Now," he said, giving me an orange, "first tell me which hand you have got that in." "The right," I said. "Now," he said, "go and stand before that glass, and tell me which hand the little girl you see there has got it in." After some perplexed contemplation, I said, "The left hand." "Exactly," he said, "and how do you explain that?" I couldn't explain it, but seeing that some solution was expected, I ventured, "If I was on the *other* side of the glass, wouldn't the orange still be in my right hand?" I can remember his laugh. "Well done, little Alice," he said. "The best answer I've had yet."[42]

While working on the early chapters of *Through the Looking-Glass* Carroll prepared a small volume of poetry, most of it previously published in magazines, which he published in January, 1869, under the title *Phantasmagoria*. The title poem deals with the unhappy experiences of a naive little ghost, but the best of the humorous poems are "Hiawatha's Photographing" (a parody of "The Song of Hiawatha"), "The Three Voices" (a parody of "The Two Voices"), and "Poeta Fit, non Nascitur" (a satire on the making of a poet).

Meanwhile, after much negotiating over meticulous details insisted upon by Carroll and Tenniel, Macmillan's published *Through the Looking-Glass* in time for Christmas, 1871. The sales were encouraging. Macmillan's first printed nine thousand copies but the public demand was such that they quickly printed an additional six thousand. The reviews were generally more enthusiastic than they had been for *Alice's Adventures in Wonderland*. The *Athenaeum*, for example, wrote that "it is with no mere book that we have to deal here ... but with the potentiality of happiness for countless children of all ages."[43]

With the masterful nonsense poem "Jabberwocky" behind him, Carroll proceeded to write the complex and more nearly perfect work of nonsense, *The Hunting of the Snark*. The last line of the poem, "For the Snark *was* Boojum you see," occurred suddenly as Carroll was strolling at Guildford in July, 1874, and he composed the final stanza several days later. At odd moments during the next two years he pieced the poem together; and

Macmillan's published the "Agony in Eight Fits," consisting
of 141 stanzas, in 1876.

He dedicated the *Snark* to Gertrude Chataway, a young girl
he first met at Sandown in 1875. As with Alice Liddell, Alice
Raikes, and many other young girls of his acquaintance, Carroll
became strongly attached to Gertrude. He later requested permission from her mother to photograph her daughter in the
nude, but the request was apparently denied. His dream-like
friendship with her, as with his other child friends, soon faded.
In 1878 he wrote to her, "So sorry you are grown-up," and two
years later to her mother, "I wonder when I shall, or whether I
ever shall, meet my (no longer little) friend again! Our friendship was very intense while it lasted—but it has gone like a
dream."[44] His feelings about Alice Liddell when she reached
puberty were similar. Nevertheless, Carroll was to revive his
friendship with Gertrude; and in 1890, when he heard that she
was ill, he wrote her a remarkable letter:

. . . Do you think a visit to the Seaside (Eastbourne) could benefit
you? And, if so, will you come and be my guest here for a while?
   I put that question *first*, advisedly: I want you just to get over
the shock of so outrageous a proposal a bit: and then you can
calmly consider what I have to say in defence of asking a young
lady of your age to be the guest of a single gentleman. First, then,
if I live to next January, I shall be 59 years old. So it's not like a man
of 30, or even a man of 40, proposing such a thing. I should hold
it quite out of the question in either case. I never thought of such a
thing myself, until 5 years ago—then, feeling I really had accumu-
lated a good lot of years, I ventured to invite a little girl of 10,
who was lent without the least demur. The next year I had one of
12 staying here for a week. The next year I invited one of 14, quite
expecting a refusal, *that* time, on the ground of her being too
old. To my surprise and delight, her mother simply wrote "Irene
may come to you for a week, or a fortnight. What day would you
like to have her?" After taking her back, I boldly invited an elder
sister of hers, aged 18. She came quite readily. I've had another
18-year-old since, and feel quite reckless now, as to ages: and, so
far as I know, "Mrs Grundy" has made no remarks at all.
   But have I had any one who is *grown-up*? (as I presume *you*
are, by this time). Well, no, I've not actually *had* one here, yet:
but I wrote the other day to invite Irene's eldest sister (who must be

23 by this time) and she writes that she can't come this year "but I shall love to come another time, if you'll ask me again!"

I would take moderately good care of you: and you should be middling well fed; and have a doctor, if you needed it, and I shouldn't allow you to talk, as that is evidently not good for you. My landlady is a good motherly creature and she and her maid would look after you well.

Another point I may as well touch on, the cost of coming. There has been a difference among my child-guests, in that respect. Some— I fancied, when I began the paragraph, that there had been one, at least, whose railway fare I had *not* paid. But I find there was none. (You see, I travelled from London *with* most of them, so it was natural to pay; though in some cases perhaps they *could* have afforded it themselves: but there were certainly *some* who couldn't have come at all, unless I had said beforehand "I will pay the journey expenses".) Therefore (with no fear that I shall offend you by so doing) I make the same offer to you.

Now, *do,* my dear child, get your parents to say "yes" (I mean supposing sea-air is good for you); and then say "yes" yourself and then tell me whether you would be competent to travel down here alone, or if I had better come to escort you.

At present there is, lying on the sofa by the open window of my tiny sitting-room, a girl-friend from Oxford, aged 17. She came yesterday, and will perhaps stay a week. After she is gone, if *you* could come for a week or longer, I should love to have you here! It would be like having my Sandown days over again![45]

The whole tone of this letter would suggest that Gertrude was still indeed a young child and not a full-grown woman. There is a striking innocence and a sense of terrible loneliness in Carroll's solicitude and persuasion, in his attempt to recreate the past ("It would be like having my Sandown days over again!"). Gertrude did come to stay at Eastboune but not until 1893. She arrived on September 19 and left on the 23rd, on which day Carroll simply recorded in his diary "Gertrude left. It has been a really delightful visit."[46]

VI   *The Noted Author*

In 1881 Carroll resigned his mathematical lectureship. Financially secure and established as an author, he noted "I shall now have my whole time at my own disposal, and, if God gives me life and continued health and strength, may hope, before my powers fail, to do some worthy work in writing—partly in the cause of Mathematical education, partly in the cause of innocent recreation for children, and partly, I hope (though so utterly unworthy of being allowed to take up such work) in the cause of religious thought."[47] But on December 8 Carroll was elected Curator of the Senior Common Room, a demanding job of housekeeping that he accepted "with no light heart."[48] He nevertheless carried out his new duties methodically and brought order to a system of accountancy that previously had been chaotic. He humorously set forth the problems of his undertaking in *Twelve Months in a Curatorship* (1884), and later, in *Three Years in a Curatorship* (1886) he discussed the ventilation, lighting, and furnishing of the Common Room under the heading "Airs, Glares and Chairs."

It was during this period that Carroll published a new collection of his verse entitled *Rhyme? and Reason?* (1883). Most of the poems were taken from *Phantasmagoria*, to which he added *The Hunting of the Snark* and a few poems hitherto unpublished. He had also been publishing a series of mathematical problems in the form of short stories in Charlotte Yonge's magazine for women, the *Monthly Packet*. In 1885 they were published together in a volume called *A Tangled Tale*.

The year 1886 was a busy one for Carroll. He worked with Macmillans' on the facsimile edition of *Alice's Adventures under Ground*, gave a series of lectures on logic at Lady Margaret Hall, worked on *Sylvie and Bruno* and *The Game of Logic*, and cooperated with Savile Clarke on the theatrical production *Alice in Wonderland*. Carroll attended the opening night's performance, December 30, at the Prince of Wales' Theatre, and recorded his observations in his diary:

The first act ('Wonderland') goes well, specially the Mad Tea Party. Mr. Sydney Harcourt is a capital 'Hatter', and Little Dorothy d'Alcourt (aet. 6 1/2) a delicious Dormouse. Phoebe Carlo is a splendid 'Alice.' Her song and dance with the Cheshire Cat (Master C. Adeson, who played the Pirate King in *Pirates of Penzance*) was a gem. The second act was flat. The two queens (two of the Rosa

Troupe) were *very* bad (as they were also in the First Act as Queen and Cook): and the 'Walrus etc,' had no definite finale. But, as a whole, the play seems a success.[49]

Later, in an essay he wrote for *The Theatre*, Carroll commented upon the performance at greater length. In his praise for Phoebe Carlo he reverts to his characteristic idealization of the Innocent Girl: "But what I admired most, as realizing most nearly my ideal heroine, was her perfect assumption of the high spirits, and readiness to enjoy *everything*, of a child out for a holiday. I doubt if any grown actress, however experienced, could have worn this air so perfectly; *we* look before and after, and sigh for what is not; a child never does *this*; and it is only a child that can utter from her heart the words poor Margaret Fuller Ossoli so longed to make her own, 'I am all happy *now.*' "[50]

During 1888 Carroll was hard at work on his *Curiosa Mathematica, Part I*, a technical analysis of Euclid's Twelfth Axiom. A less abstruse but more interesting project was his *The Nursery Alice*, a shortened version of *Alice's Adventures in Wonderland* for children below the age of five. Published in 1889, the work contained twenty of Tenniel's illustrations, enlarged and colored. Carroll explained in his preface that "my ambition *now* is (is it a vain one?) to be read by Children aged from Nought to Five. To be read? Nay, not so! Say rather to be thumbed, to be cooed over, to be dogs'-eared, to be rumpled, to be kissed, by the illiterate, ungrammatical, dimpled Darlings, that fill your Nursery with merry uproar...."[51]

Carroll finally completed his novel *Sylvie and Bruno* and published it in December, 1889. Its sequel, *Sylvie and Bruno Concluded*, appeared in December, 1893. The work fell far short of the success of the two Alice books, a fact due in part to the heavy moralistic tone and in part to the difficult theory that man may go through three stages in relation to the supernatural. Nevertheless, by 1890 Carroll's reputation was secure and a reviewer could not blithely dismiss his latest work. The *Athenaeum* was fairly generous in its review of *Sylvie and Bruno*: "Being written by Mr. Lewis Carroll, it is needless to say that it is full of amusing things, and not without some of 'the graver thoughts of human life'; nevertheless it falls far below 'Alice in Wonderland,' and the illustrations by Mr. Harry Furniss are by no means worthy of his reputation." It is remarkable that the reviewer goes on to say that the characters Sylvie and Bruno are "from first to last ... delightful."[52]

Although Carroll enjoyed the fame which he acquired after the publication of the Alice books, in his old age he scrupulously avoided public attention. He denied requests for autographs and to all but children would be recognized only as Charles Dodgson. When Alexander Macmillan invited Carroll to a publisher's party he received this response: "Many thanks for your kind intimation of the days of your 'receptions' in Bedford Street: but (how many 'buts' there are in life!) I fear that in such an assembly it would be almost impossible to preserve an incognito. I cannot of course help there being many people who know the connection between my real name and my 'alias,' but the fewer there are who are able to connect my face with the name of 'Lewis Carroll' the happier for me. So I hope you will kindly excuse my nonappearance."[53]

Toward the end of his life Carroll acquired a reputation as a preacher in Oxford, Guildford, and Eastbourne. His stammer, of course, continued to make his speaking in public an ordeal. In a letter to a friend he confided his anxiety: "A sermon would be quite formidable enough for me, even if I did *not* suffer from the physical difficulty of hesitation, but with *that* super-added, the prospect is sometimes almost too much for my nerves."[54] He nevertheless was apparently happy in his ministry. After he preached his first sermon at Eastbourne he wrote, "I am very thankful to have had this opportunity of work."[55] The text of his sermon was "Lead us not into temptation."

Throughout the Alice books there are many references to death, from Alice's fear of killing someone if she drops the jar of marmalade to the threat to Alice's life by the Red King's awaking. And in *The Hunting of the Snark* there is the theme of annihilation. In his sixty-fourth year Carroll, anticipating his own death three years later, wrote to one of his sisters, "It is getting increasingly difficult now to remember *which* of one's friends remain alive, and *which* have gone 'into the land of the great departed, into the silent land.' Also, such news comes less and less as a shock, and more and more one realizes that it is an experience each of *us* has to face before long. That fact is getting *less* dreamlike to me now, and I sometimes think what a grand thing it will be to be able to say to oneself, 'Death is *over* now; there is not *that* experience to be faced again."[56] In 1898 Carroll developed a serious bronchial infection and on January 14, at 2:00 p.m., he died at "The Chestnuts," Guildford.

CHAPTER 2

Early Nonsense

I "The Walking-Stick of Destiny"

CARROLL'S brilliant genius for nonsense did not spring full blown with the Alice books. It has been seen in his childhood games at Croft and, more developed, is apparent in his literary and artistic productions for *The Rectory Umbrella* and *Mischmasch*. As Florence Milner points out, "it was through editing these little magazines and doing most of the work upon them himself that he made his first semi-formal approach to literature and art."[1] It was the plan that all members of the Dodgson family should contribute; but as their enthusiasm waned, Carroll was left with the whole task. He furnished all material for *The Rectory Umbrella* and all but two poems for *Mischmasch*. One of the stories in *The Rectory Umbrella*, "The Walking-Stick of Destiny," is remarkable for its unusual and sophisticated treatment of the short story form and reveals the genius that Carroll had acquired for nonsense by his eighteenth birthday. (The concept of nonsense used in this book is explained in detail in Chapter 3, section II. Let it suffice to say at this point that the term signifies a self-contained verbal structure and that "meaning" can be derived solely in terms of that structure.)

The story, comprised of eight brief chapters and seventy-five footnotes, purports to be a mystery. The Baron Slogdod is anxiously pacing his chamber when Signor Blowski arrives to deliver a letter from Baron Muggzwig. Slogdod offers Blowski a goblet of wine (apparently poisoned) but Blowski quietly exchanges his goblet for Slogdod's. The first chapter ends with Slogdod, very much alive, hurling Blowski out the window as his response to Muggzwig's letter.

The scene then shifts to the cave of a magician who, in the midst of concocting an elaborate potion or charm (composed of one thousand ingredients), is interrupted by the sudden arrival of a bruised Signor Blowski. Blowski wants the magician's advice on his recent unfortunate adventure with Slogdod but renders his story in such a confused and general manner (in order to disguise his own hand in the affair) that the magician is utterly nonplussed and can only reply, "yes, yes, my lad, *you're* in for it."[2] What he is in for the reader has not the slightest idea—although, as destiny would have it, it turns out that in the last chapter, Blowski was indeed in for it.

Meanwhile Slogdod's footman is serving his master more wine, the Baron's meals consisting of nothing but hot, spiced wine (as one learns in a footnote). After his repast he looks out upon the spot where Blowski earlier had been thrown and sees a mysterious figure lurking in the area. The chapter ends with Slogdod saying, "I do wonder who that is" (p. 19).

Before too long another visitor arrives at the Slogdod household, a Mr. Milton Smith, presumably an Englishman to pepper the international flavor the story has acquired from the names of the other characters. He introduces himself to Slogdod as a poet and begins to describe the "gorgeous rusticity" of the surroundings in iambic tetrameter couplets. Slogdod occasionally pitches in with an appropriately outrageous rhyme. The Baron invites the poet to spend the night and then retires. The poet, however, goes to the window and pulls up a rope ladder produced by the mysterious stranger seen earlier by the Baron.

The scene switches back again to the magician's cave. The magician is in the process of writing an "awful spell" upon a magic scroll suspended from the mouth of a viper, upon whom is seated an owl. To either side of the owl is a black cat ("a left-hand cat" and "a right-hand cat"). An "animated potatoe" hovers over the mystic scroll. Weird sounds and sights manifest themselves in the cave; and when they finally subside all that remains is the scroll, a pen, sealing wax, and a lighted taper. The magician then exclaims, "August potatoe, I obey your potent voice" (p. 44), and summons a courier to dispatch the scroll. It is not noted in the text where the document is to be taken but an accompanying illustration depicts the courier carrying the scroll and upon it is written "To Signor Blowski."

The next chapter returns to Slogdod's home where Milton Smith and the mysterious stranger are in the act of stealing the

Baron's strongbox, which turns out to contain nothing but a walking stick. The mysterious stranger, disgusted at the paltry contents, is convinced that Muggzwig, who hired both men to steal the box, will not be pleased with a mere walking stick. The poet, however, delivers his find to Muggzwig, who rewards the hireling with a purse of gold. The chapter closes with Muggzwig muttering, "nothing is now wanting but the toad" (p. 59), a statement curiously like the magician's, "Now for the toad," which concluded the previous chapter.

In the penultimate chapter the reader learns that Baron Muggzwig is fat, possessed of an obtuse intellect, and speaks in near incomprehensible run-on sentences. He is visited by the mysterious stranger and the magician, who have come to see if Muggzwig has acquired the walking stick and what he wants done with Signor Blowski. Muggzwig's reply consists of a 228-word sentence (which he never completes, for his visitors finally leave the room) that merely aggravates the confusion that already abounds in the reader's mind.

At this point the reader may be expected to have gathered together several questions, all of which, one may hope, will be answered in the final chapter of the story. Why does Muggzwig want Slogdod's walking stick? Why is the stick so valuable that the rather impoverished Slogdod keeps it locked in a strongbox? What roles do Blowski, Smith, the mysterious stranger, and the magician really play in the adventure? What is the relationship between the above characters and Muggzwig? What has happened to Blowski? Why did the mysterious stranger 1) arrive at Muggzwig's home in the company of the magician, with whom he has not previously been associated and 2) bother to go to Muggzwig's at all, since earlier he was disappointed at the discovery of the walking stick in the strongbox and left Smith to deliver it to Muggzwig? Why did the magician have the magic scroll delivered to Blowski, and for what purpose was he preparing the elaborate potion? What is Slogdod's reaction when he discovers that his walking stick has been stolen? These, then, are some of the major questions which the story has raised (there are numerous minor ones which, in the interests of space, will not be discussed).

The final chapter introduces an encouraging footnote. "This

chapter, it is hoped, will clear up all the mystery in the story" (p. 75). The scene presents Baron Slogdod seated in the hall of his ancestors, seven thousand witnesses staring intently at him. Sitting upon a table before the Baron is a hideous magic toad (which recalls the earlier remarks made by the magician and Muggzwig). Everyone present fears and loathes the toad except Slogdod, who gives it a "sportive kick." The final paragraph of the story belongs to the magician, who exclaims: "The man I accuse, if man indeed he be, is—Blowski!" At those words the shrunken form of Blowski appears, opens its mouth to speak but issues no sound. Then the magician pronounces the fatal words: "Recreant vagabond! misguided reprobate! receive thy due deserts!" (Shades of the trial of the Knave of Hearts). The form sinks silently to the ground, all is momentarily darkness, and the returning light reveals "a heap of mashed potatoe. . . . a globular form faintly loomed through the darkness, and howled once audibly, then all was still. Reader, our tale is told." A footnote after "potatoe" comments: "Many have vainly asked the author, 'What had he done?' He didn't know" (p. 77).

Nothing is resolved, all of the questions raised by the story remain unanswered. What, then, is the story supposed to be all about? It is about itself, the short story as a self-contained game that pays minimal attention to references and rules outside itself. The numerous red herrings have been introduced into the story for their own sake—they are the story. The conventional expectations one brings to the reading of a story are at almost every turn frustrated. The familiar sequence of events that characterizes everyday life and the traditional structure of a mystery story (from ignorance to enlightenment) are deliberately undermined. The fun of the story consists of the tension that arises between order and disorder, between expectation and frustration.

The reader's demand for unity is countered by a series of discrete events that defy fusion while implying its possibility. For example, the recurrent references to the toad would seem to offer an explanation of the toad that appears in the last chapter—but all one can say, alas, is a toad is a toad. Ambiguity may be the cordial of fiction and poetry, but it is deadly poison to nonsense. The footnote in chapter 5 informs the reader that "the potatoe's history should be carefully remembered, as it is important" (p. 42). Indeed, it is important, inasmuch as at the conclusion of the story it appears as a heap of mashed potato that displaces the ghost of Blowski. But its importance beyond that cannot be assessed. Accretive significance, like ambiguity, is destructive of nonsense. Many of the other footnotes provide cross references but the references do not explain each other; rather, they simply add disparate details or reiterate what is already clear. The various multiplications of relationships throughout the story are consistently inhibited, whereas a badly written mystery may introduce red herrings haphazardly to disguise a poorly conceived structure. Thus, for example, the sudden appearance of the magician as a cohort of the mysterious stranger and accuser of Blowski cannot be explained according to traditional story logic. But in terms of this specific story and its nonsense structure the actions of the magician are as consistent and logical as those of the other characters.

It should be clear that any attempt to analyze the story for its "submerged meaning" would be fruitless. "The Walking-Stick of Destiny" offers a satisfying literary experience by treating the short story form as a word game to be played between the author and his reader. Carroll has Muggzwig and the magician both accuse Blowski. Why?, and of what?, the reader demands to know. Simply because that is what they do. They have no motivation because Carroll gave them none. Likewise, Blowski has committed a crime only because his accusers imply that he has, because he is the kind of victim that Franz Kafka has rediscovered in our century. The reader is thus left with an "absolute" fiction, with little to draw upon from everyday life or from the traditional story to help him through the seeming maze of absurdity. "The Walking-Stick of Destiny," of course, as a work of nonsense, pales next to Carroll's achievement in the Alice books, which transcend such heavy-handed devices as footnotes to highlight the nonsense. Nevertheless, this early story clearly marks Carroll's development from a skilled apprentice at red herrings to a master of nonsense.

II "The Vernon Gallery"

Carroll included in *The Rectory Umbrella* several delightful skits on pictures "in the Vernon Gallery," with caricatures of the work of Sir Joshua Reynolds, John Frederick Herring, William Collins, Sir David Wilkie, Sir Augustus Ward Callcott, Sir Edwin Landseer, and William Etty. The Vernon Gallery was a collection of English paintings founded by Robert Vernon at South Kensington. Carroll was apparently interested in the collection, and his parodies demonstrate the sort of humor that makes the Alice books famous. The first painting has the following simple comment: " 'The Age of Innocence,' by Sir. J. Reynolds, representing a young Hippopotamus seated under a shady tree, presents to the contemplative mind a charming union of youth and innocence."[3] Reynolds' "The Age of Innocence," now in the National Gallery, presents a young girl seated beneath a pair of crossed trees (Carroll's hippo is seated beneath a similar pair of trees), her hands clasped to her breast and looking very much like the many girls Carroll was to befriend, write about, and photograph. There is an artificiality in her frozen posture of innocence that uncannily anticipates Carroll's own songs of innocence and numerous photographs that sentimentalize young girls. In retaining the background of Reynolds' picture and replacing the girl with a grinning hippopotamus whose bulk nearly fills the foreground Carroll achieves the outrageous effects of nonsense and parody.

Most of the sketches and comments from Carroll's "The Vernon Gallery" caricature the anecdotal paintings of the Victorian period, those that depict scenes of everyday life with a moral, pathetic, or comical twist to them. "The Scanty Meal," for example, attributed to Herring, makes fun of the sentimental pictures showing the hard times experienced by the poor. In this instance, the serving man announces to a middle-class family seated at the table, "Please'm, cook says there's only a billionth of an ounce of bread left, and she must keep that for next week!" (p. 13).

In cartoon-balloon fashion each member of the family responds to the dire news with a concern for the mathematics of the occasion rather than for their hunger. A spectacled old woman, for example, exclaims: "I must really get stronger glasses, this is the second nonillionth I've not seen." Carroll comments that he "can trace in the eye of the . . . lady a lurking suspicion that her glasses are not really in fault, and that the old gentleman has

helped her to *nothing* instead of a nonillionth" (p. 14). In a footnote he explains a nonillionth as 1/000000000000000000000000.

The third painting is "The Woodland Gait," in which Carroll
pokes fun at Collins' formulaic and sentimental depiction of
rural life. As T. S. R. Boase has observed, Collins' "Woods and
hedgerows, the background to his urchins swinging on gates or
his villagers proceeding to church, could at times degenerate
into dull formulas."[4] Carroll's drawing is a crude cartoon of a
country dance, which allows him the pun on "gate," gates being
a trademark of Collins' rural scenes.

"The First Earring" mocks Wilkie's paintings of domestic
scenes and shows a gruff fat man pulling a schoolboy by the
ear. To avoid any ambiguity Carroll footnotes "earring" in his
text—"a pulling by the ear" (p. 30). This play with language and
logic is evident throughout the caricatures, including "The
Wooden Bridge" (Calcott), which depicts four farm boys trying to force an obstinate pig across a wooden bridge. The back
legs of the pig are tied and a boy has one of the fore-legs in
his grasp. It thus appears, Carroll argues, "either the height of
cruelty or insanity to expect it to walk across on one leg." He
footnotes "walk": "The word (walk) implies the use of more
legs than one. The only way it could possibly advance would
be hopping" (p. 40). As in "The Scanty Meal," the absurdity
arises from shifting the issues from hunger to mathematics in
the one case, and from logistics to linguistics in the other. This
digressionary technique is basic to nonsense and will be seen
skillfully developed in the *Alice* books.

"High Life and Low Life" (Landseer) and "The Duett"
(Etty) complete the Vernon Gallery. The former satirizes the
social statement of Victorian paintings by showing a gardener
with a whip chasing a group of lower-class boys from his
orchard. Two boys have reached safety over the wall, but one
is suspended from the wall by a nail that caught his coat and
another lies prone and flattened under a basket full of apples.
Carroll comments, "One can trace in it, besides fear of the
approaching gardener, a shade of sorrow and regret for the
basket of apples he has just dropped. His companion, however,
whose face is just visible from under the basket, probably
feels more *real* sorrow for that event" (p. 54).

"The Duett" brings the stylized, almost Pre-Raphaelite style down to earth by having the luxuriously coiffured lady play a pair of common kitchen bellows, "the only instrument by means of which a brisk air can be produced" (p. 68). It is doubtful that one could have derived the pun by merely examining the drawing.

III *Zoological Papers*

The animal world always held a fascination for Carroll; and in a series of sketches called "Zoological Papers," printed in *The Rectory Umbrella*, he displays a whimsical bestiary suggestive of the zany animal creatures of Wonderland. The first paper deals with pixies: "the best description we can collect of them is this, that they are a species of fairies about two feet high, of small and graceful figure; they are covered with a dark reddish sort of fur; the general expression of their faces is sweetness and good humour; the former quality is probably the reason why foxes are so fond of eating them."[5] Carroll's typical wit is seen in the equation of a sweet appearance and a sweet taste and in the outrageous idea that these legendary sprites are devoured by foxes.

The next paper discusses the Australian parrot known as the Lory. This exotic bird intrigued Carroll, for he was later to include it in *Alice's Adventures in Wonderland,* where it represented Lorina Liddell. In the "Zoological Papers" he invests the creature with a certain mythological and literary significance. Associated with Robert Southey's "The Curse of Kehama," the Lory had an extraordinary origin: "The time and place of the Lory's birth is uncertain: the egg from which it was hatched was most probably, to judge from the colour of the bird, one of those magnificent Easter eggs which our readers have doubtless often seen; the experiment of hatching an Easter egg is at any rate worth trying" (p. 23).

"Fishs" are the subject of the third paper. Found only in Germany and characterized by their angles, they are not to be confused, Carroll warns, with the English "fishes." Here is part of Carroll's description of "fishs": "They are wonderfully light, and have a sort of beak or snout of a metallic substance: as this is solid, and they have no other mouth, their hollowness is thus easily accounted for. The colour is sticky and comes off on the fingers, and they can swim back downward just as easily as in the usual way" (p. 35). By dropping the "e" from "fishes," a plural form appropriate in certain instances, Carroll creates a group of mythological creatures. "Fishs" does not exist as a word; and it is therefore only fitting, in the logic of nonsense, that the characteristics of "fishs" be absurd.

The last paper, "The One-Winged Dove," is the most amusing in the series. It opens with the logic of Wonderland:

All the information we can collect on this subject is taken from an advertisement in *The Times*, July 2, 1850, the rest is conjecture.

To begin with the advertisement, "The One-Winged Dove must die, unless the Crane returns to be a shield against her enemies." From this we draw the following facts. (1) It is a dove with one wing. (2) The Crane is its friend. (3) It has enemies who wish its death. (4) The Crane alone can resist these enemies. (5) The Crane has left it. (6) (from the mere fact of the advertisement being sent to *The Times*) The Dove can write. (7) (from the same fact) The Crane can read. (8) (do.) The Dove has more than 12s. in the world. (9) (do.) The Crane takes in *The Times*." (p. 46)

The essay goes on to explore these "facts" and deduces that the Dove's enemy are "fishs": "The Dove, we know, is talented: it therefore probably writes in *Punch*: 'fishs' have 'angles': 'angle' is a word of two meanings. What so natural, then, as that it should write jokes on 'fishs'? This would of course enrage the said 'fishs,' and enmity would thereby arise" (p. 48).

Many of Carroll's other early prose works, while mildly entertaining, do not exhibit his premature genius for nonsense and the absurd. "Crundle Castle" (c. 1850), "Wilhelm Von Schmitz" (1854), "Photography Extraordinary" (1855), and "A Photographer's Day Out" (1860) might have been written by almost any intelligent young man. There is, however, in "Photography Extraordinary" a zany device that might have interested the White Knight or the professor in *Sylvie and Bruno*. Carroll's fascination with gadgets and inventions finds vent here in a fantastic photographic device. A young man's brain, functioning like a camera lens, has its thoughts transposed to special photographic paper. Upon the first development, the paper reveals a style of thought characteristic of the "Milk-and-Water School of Novels." Further developments of the paper have the thoughts evolve through the "Matter-of-Fact School" to the "Spasmodic or German School." The role of machines and gadgets was to expand in Carroll's later, more sophisticated nonsense. Technology may have frightened the Romantics but Carroll gracefully incorporated the machinery of his day into his writings and transformed it through fantasy into his peculiar romantic vision of the world.

CHAPTER 3

Poetry

I *Serious Verse*

LEWIS Carroll's serious poetry is very dull. Most of his comic verse on the other hand, is generally amusing and sometimes exhibits a genius that remains unrivaled. Nonsense poems such as "Jabberwocky," "The Walrus and the Carpenter," and *The Hunting of the Snark,* and parodies like "You are old, Father William," "Speak roughly to your little boy," and "Twinkle, twinkle, little Bat" are inspired works that have become an integral part of our literary and popular culture. The gulf between his serious and humorous poetry is as vast as that between Carroll the Oxford don and Carroll the creator of Alice. Although the focus of this chapter will be upon his humorous verse and its development into pure nonsense, it may be helpful in understanding Carroll's growth as a nonsense poet to look first at his conventional verse.

Most of Carroll's serious verse appeared as part of the first edition of *Phantasmagoria* (1869) and was reissued in 1898 in *Three Sunsets.* One of the recurring themes of these poems is the loss of innocence or love. The "Three Sunsets," for example, deals with a man who has known "the star of perfect womanhood," a creature who made him bless the world "where there could be / So beautiful a thing as she." But then the two lovers bid farewell and time begins to wreak its havoc upon the man:

> So after many years he came
> A wanderer from a distant shore:
> The street, the house, were still the same,
> But those he sought were there no more:
> His burning words, his hopes and fears,
> Unheeded fell on alien ears.

> Only the children from their play
> Would pause the mournful tale to hear,
> Shrinking in half-alarm away,
> Or, step by step would venture near
> To touch with timid curious hands
> That strange wild man from other lands.[1]

Cast out of his romantic paradise, the lover is now alienated from the real world, with which he refuses to compromise. Tennyson, of course, in section VII of *In Memoriam* describes this emotion much more forcefully: "Dark house, by which once more I stand / Here in the long unlovely street, / Doors, where my heart was used to beat / So quickly, waiting for a hand." Carroll's images are rather abstract and his meter uninteresting. Tennyson's skillfully placed caesuras and surprising adjectives like "unlovely" strengthen his lines.

Carroll's poem continues with the theme of "Mariana" and "The Palace of Art," namely, that emotional self-indulgence is spiritually and psychologically destructive. Sounding very much like Mariana, the lover sighs, "She will not come to-day"; and he proceeds to invent "new luxuries of agony." Carroll's didacticism gradually emerges: "So all his manhood's strength and pride / One sickly dream had swept aside." Finally, his lover does indeed return to him but he was "Too rapt in selfish grief to hear / even when happiness was near," and thus he dies despising the present and powerless to recapture the past. One suspects, without Tennyson needing to tell us, that Mariana's grief was equally self-indulgent and that her lover's return would spoil the luxury of her gloom. Carroll simply could not resist the impulse to set the moral record straight. But even Tennyson, in "The Palace of Art," heavy-handedly condemns the immorality of selfish estheticism. What is interesting about both poets, however, is that they are fascinated by and drawn to those very emotions that their rational selves distrust. Carroll, for example, freely indulged himself in wistful memories of the "island farm" of his childhood without any recrimination. "Three Sunsets" simply demonstrates that the past, when it consumes the present, is dangerous and potentially destructive.

"The Valley of the Shadow of Death," on the other hand, affirms the healing power of the past. An old man on his death bed tells his son the story of how he was rescued from despair by happy, innocent cottage children who were reading from the Bible "Come unto Me, come unto Me— / All ye that labour, come unto Me— / Ye heavy-laden, come to Me— / And I will give you rest" (p. 415). This event not only redeemed his dark day but continues to strengthen his prospects for the future, as he can now interpret his passing years as "home-ward-speeding" towards his departed wife: "So with a glad and patient heart / I move toward mine end." The poem never makes clear what caused the old man to despair in the first place. There were simply "evil spells that held me thrall" (the language suggests "La Belle Dame Sans Merci" and may imply sexual anxiety). The movement from suicidal thoughts ("What need to lag and linger on / Till life be cold and gray?") to affirmation of life ("Blest day!") is similar to that in Tennyson's "The Two Voices," where the sight of a happy family going to church enables the poet to repress the barren voice for one that proclaims "Rejoice! Rejoice!" "The Valley of the Shadow of Death" serves as a companion poem to "Three Sunsets" in that one shows the past to be redemptive and the other to be destructive, the former associated with child-like innocence, the latter with romantic eroticism.

In his poem "Solitude" Carroll makes a wistful attempt to recapture the lost innocence of his childhood. In a pensive mood the poet retreats to a silent woods: "Here from the world I win release, / Nor scorn of men, nor footstep rude, / Break in to mar the holy peace / Of this great solitude" (p. 417). He glories in the memories of "Life's young spring, / Of innocence, of love and truth!" and concludes: "I'd give all wealth that years have piled, / The slow result of Life's decay, / To be once more a little child / For one Bright summer-day." Carroll was only twenty-one when he wrote these lines, a fairly typical age for a poet to write his "old age" poem. Keenly aware of the passage of time and mortality, Carroll relentlessly sought refuge from decay in memories of golden fairy lands, in photography, and in constantly associating himself with children.

"Beatrice" sets forth the theme that youthful innocence can control and structure the violence and disorder of experience. Beatrice, the "sainted, ethereal maid," can tame a wild beast:

> For I think, if a grim wild beast
> Were to come from his charnel-cave,
> From his jungle-home in the East—
> Stealthily creeping with bated breath,
> Stealthily creeping with eyes of death—
> He would all forget his dream of the feast,
> And crouch at her feet a slave. (p. 420)

These lines, richly romantic in sentiment, suggest that innocence is a stay not only against a violent eroticism but against mortality—and perhaps those two forces are related in Carroll's mind. Beatrice has the same powers as Robert Browning's Pippa, whose song enabled Sebald to repent his crimes of murder and lust:

> And be sure, if a savage heart,
> In a mask of human guise,
> Were to come on her here apart—
> Bound for a dark and a deadly deed,
> Hurrying past with pitiless speed—
> He would suddenly falter and guiltily start
> At the glance of her pure blue eyes.

The entire poem is, of course, sentimental—most of the innocents in Carroll's serious verse are emblems of abstract forces that perform almost magical feats in the real world, such as thwarting murderous erotic crimes or preserving the hope of despairing old men.

Another sentimental poem, "Stolen Waters," resembles Keats's "La Belle Dame Sans Merci" with the addition of a happy ending. Christina Rossetti's "Goblin Market" appeared the year Carroll wrote his poem and well may have influenced it. A lithe, tall, and fair maiden, possessing sinister powers, offers the narrator (a knight) the juice of "rarest fruitage": "I drank the juice; and straightway felt / A fire within my brain: / My soul within me seemed to melt / In sweet delirious pain" (p. 423). "Youth is the season to rejoice," the maiden counsels, and lures the knight into her dark dream of sexual pleasure: "The very heart from out my breast / I plucked, I gave it willingly: / Her very heart she gave to me— / Then died the glory from the west." Upon his commitment to her, the horrific effects of time and

mortality blight his dream: "In the gray light I saw her face, /
And it was withered, old, and gray; / The flowers were fading
in their place, / Were fading with the fading day." He flees
from the fatal lady, senses that his heart has turned to stone,
and longs to die in order to be released from his misery. But,
as in "The Valley of the Shadow of Death," the narrator hears a
voice that renews his hope: " 'Be as a child— / So shalt thou
sing for very joy of breath— / So shalt thou wait thy dying, /
In holy transport lying.' "

As in some of the previous poems, eroticism triggers in the
mind of the narrator the horrors of time, decay, and death. John
Skinner notes that Carroll "offers a solution to the insoluble
dilemma of adulthood by substituting a state of childish existence, aimed not at the realization of a mature adult life, but
fixed at a level of innocence in life until the adult-child passes
into the larger innocence of death."[2] The fascination with
erotic love and the impulse to repress it coexist in Carroll's
verse and, possibly, according to Hudson, in his life as well:

He was a man who carried his childhood with him; the love
that he understood and longed for was a protective love. He had a
deep instinctive admiration for women, yearning for their sympathy
and often finding it. But it is possible that he could not reconcile
in himself love and desire, and likely that he avoided problems
of adult love and intimacy in his own life because he knew that he
was pulled in two different ways (ambivalence is the modern term),
and that in any close relationship something compelled him to seek
distance and detachment.[3]

In "Faces in the Fire" the poet anticipates his lonely future
and idealizes a lost but haunting love. Curiously, this love from
his past does not sweep away "all his manhood's strength and
pride" as it did in "Three Sunsets." The romantic melancholy
of the poem is real but it is not portrayed as destructive. In
fact, there is a kind of pleasurable brooding over the lost innocent: "Oh, Time was young, and Life was warm, / When first I
saw that fairy-form, / Her dark hair tossing in the storm" (p.
437). She has since aged, he recognizes, "And she is strange
and far away / That might have been mine own to-day." A. L.
Taylor believes that the idealized woman of the poem is Alice

Liddell.[4] Alice was four years old when Carroll first met her and seven and a half in 1860, when he wrote the poem. If Taylor is correct and Alice is indeed the "little childish form," then she is merely imagined to have "locks of jet . . . turned to gray." Taylor's assumption would help to explain why the love relationship in this poem is not threatening or destructive but simply wistful and melancholy. The "aged Alice" is as safe and beautiful as Keats's unravished bride of silence. She is a haunting face in the fire, a memory stirred from Carroll's recollection of the distant paradise of his own childhood: "An island farm— broad seas of corn / Stirred by the wandering breath of morn— / The happy spot where I was born." And if his lover's face vanishes among the "dust and ashes white," leaving him alone in the darkness, at least it is a love he can indulge and understand, one that has been purged of eroticism.

S. D. Collingwood recognized the unhappiness and anxiety that Carroll revealed in his volume *Three Sunsets*: "One cannot read this little volume without feeling that the shadow of some disappointment lay over Lewis Carroll's life. Such I believe to have been the case, and it was this that gave him his wonderful sympathy with all who suffered. But those who loved him would not wish to lift the veil from those dead sanctities, nor could any purpose be served by doing so."[5]

II *Humorous Verse: The Ascendency of Nonsense*

Elizabeth Sewell in her book *The Field of Nonsense*[6] has provided the most perceptive and comprehensive analysis of nonsense to date. Since this chapter will be largely devoted to Carroll's nonsense verse, some of Sewell's observations will be summarized to provide the framework for much of the discussion to follow. The world of nonsense, she contends, is a universe not of things but of words and ways of using them. The straight-forward, unambiguous nature of nonsense is usually reinforced by the use of pictorial illustration. Nonsense is by nature logical and antipoetic and is an attempt to render language as a closed and consistent system on its own. It reorganizes language, not according to the rules of prose or poetry, but according to those of play; and the objects of that play are words. Since what is highly variable cannot be played with, ambiguity must be stripped as far as possible from the language. Nonsense works with discrete units, or words, and organizes them within a strict self referential framework (a Boojum is a Boojum). Nonsense disorders references that words have to the familiar sequence of events in everyday life. The defining characteristic of the game of nonsense, then, is the order-disorder dialect in the mind. Just when a line or passage of nonsense begins to make sense (that is, to be relatable to the everyday world), that sense is cancelled by a subsequent passage that demands one not go outside of the work, outside of the language, for an explanation. The natural tendency of a reader is to ask, what does this line mean? The answer, in nonsense, is that it means what it says and no interpretations apply. If Sewell is correct in her analysis, then countless interpretations of the allegorical and symbolic meanings of works such as *The Hunting of the Snark* are impositions upon a work that steadfastly begrudges and denies any consistent "reading." She is probably right. When it comes to the prose works, however, she is on more dangerous grounds—for as she recognizes, "it may be that Nonsense goes better in verse than in prose."[7] There are obviously many aspects of the Alice books that do relate to the everyday life of both Victorian England and our own day.

Thus nonsense selects and organizes words in such a way as to frustrate the mind's tendency to multiply relationships. The nonsense universe must be the sum of its parts and nothing more, the emphasis always being upon the parts and not the whole; for there must be no fusion or synthesis. As an aid in inhibiting imagination and ambiguity, nonsense is usually accompanied by illustrations. As Sewell observes, "they sterilize the mind's powers of invention and combination of images while seeming to nourish it, and by precision and detail they contribute towards detachment and definition of the elements of the Nonsense universe."[8] In summary, she asserts that "all the finer points of the Nonsense game . . . contribute to the main aim: to create a universe which will be logical and orderly, with separate units held together by a strict economy of relations, not subject to dream and disorder with its multiplication of relationships and associations."[9]

It may now be clearer, in retrospect, why Carroll's serious verse is so unsatisfactory. It is the product of a clear and logical mind that shuns the richness of ambiguity and symbolism. At his serious best, Carroll writes lines that resemble in diction and prosody second-rate neo-classical poetry. His romantic impulses are carefully organized, controlled, and submerged through the use of regular meters, strict rhymes, and conventional, often hackneyed, phrases, so that finally there is no feeling, no mystery, that emerges from the work. But exactly those qualities of mind—meticulousness, logicality, orderliness—that hamper Carroll as a serious poet enable him to be the genius of nonsense. He delights equally in puzzles, numbers, and words; and his most elaborate fantasies are as carefully controlled as a mathematical process. His nonsense, according to Sewell, makes him "a central figure, as important for England, and in the same way, as Mallarmé is for France."[10] Such authors as T. S. Eliot, James Joyce, Franz Kafka, and Wallace Stevens are all practitioners of nonsense, and in a sense one may see in Carroll's nonsense the roots of much twentieth-century literature.

a.   Juvenilia

Very little attention has been given to Carroll's early humorous verse. Much of it is obviously inferior to his later work, but an examination of his youthful attempts at humor will reveal his development into a poet of nonsense. As W. H. Auden pointed out, Carroll was greatly aided in his development as a writer by having an audience with which he was intimate and in which he had no literary rival.[11] Carroll therefore was assured of an immediate and personal response to his works, usually from family and friends of the rectory; for most of his early writings and drawings appeared in family magazines such as *The Rectory Umbrella, Mischmasch,* and *Useful and Instructive Poetry.* Although many of the pieces which appeared in these family productions were slight, the approval and applause of his family and friends greatly strengthened and reinforced Carroll's determination to continue to amuse those surrounding him, particularly the children.

The first of the family magazines was *Useful and Instructive Poetry,* written about the year 1845, when Carroll was only

thirteen years old. Some of the humorous verses show that he was
remarkably precocious. "Rules and Regulations" pokes fun at
copybook maxims:

> Learn well your grammar,
> and never stammer,
> Write well and neatly,
> And sing most sweetly.
>
> . . . .
>
> Drink tea, not coffee;
> Never eat toffy.
> Eat bread with butter.
> Once more, don't stutter.
>
> . . . .
>
> Starve your canaries.
> Believe in fairies.
> If you are able,
> Don't have a stable
> With any mangers.
> Be rude to strangers.
> *Moral*: Behave[12]

Still a far cry from the pure nonsense of *The Hunting of the
Snark*, this early piece nevertheless anticipates the later nonsense in several particulars. One of the characteristics of nonsense noted by Sewell is what she calls a "thing series": "Anything can go into the thing series provided that the list when
drawn up will defeat the dream tendency of the mind to run
things together." "Rules and Regulations" sets forth an incon-
gruous list of social commandments that the moral, Behave,
simply cannot synthesize, except as a joke. Many of the rules
are dictated solely by the requirements of rhyme, not reason:
"never eat toffy" is an auditory corollary of "Drink tea, not
coffee." In a sense, rules are arbitrary whether formulated by a
disciplinarian or by the necessity of rhyme. In any event, the
emphasis in the poem is clearly upon the parts and not upon the
whole. Furthermore, there is no ambiguity in any of the lines.
It may make no ordinary sense to be told to starve one's
canaries, but there certainly is no question about the single meaning of the command. The poem comes close to being pure nonsense in that it does create a logical and orderly (helped by

the couplets and regular meter) program of behavior, with distinct units (incongruously welded together by the couplets), not subject to the disorder occasioned by the multiplication of relationships and associations. Some of the lines, however, refer clearly to one's everyday world and make conventional sense, such as the first four lines quoted above. The reference to stammering, in fact, derives from Carroll's own speech difficulty. The entire poem makes an implicit reference to the real world of maxims and moral precepts, although, as with a parody, the poem may still have a life of its own, perhaps a limited one, even when not read in the context of the work it pokes fun at.

Another poem from *Useful and Instructive Poetry* which illustrates some of the principles of nonsense achieved at this early date is "Brother and Sister."[13] A brother peremptorily orders his sister to go to bed, to which she replies, "Do you want a battered hide, / Or scratches to your face applied?" The brother then resorts to a greater threat: "I'd make you into mutton broth / As easily as kill a moth!" She dares him to do so, and he runs to the cook for a frying pan. The cook asks him what he needs one for, and he answers, "I wish to make an Irish stew." When she discovers that the boy's sister will be the meat, she refuses to lend him her pan, and the poem ends with the moral, "Never stew your sister." The poem resists any "interpretation" and could be passed off as simply silly. As with many of Carroll's famous angry and ill-tempered characters, such as the Duchess and the Red Queen, the aggressive behavior of the brother seems gratuitous. Furthermore, his attempt to implement his verbal threat of stewing his sister into mutton broth suggests a literal mindedness that comes as a surprise, horrific and comic at once. There is a great deal of hostility and aggressiveness throughout Carroll's writings, and it is particularly refreshing to find those qualities in poems and stories about children; for it leads away from the conventional pietistic treatment of childhood that grew out of the romantic period and flourished in the Victorian era. The poem's moral, never stew your sister, follows as night follows day. The cook's refusal to lend the boy a frying pan terminates the boy's cannibalistic plan and forces the moral.

Psychoanalytical critics, such as Phyllis Greenacre, have observed that the theme of oral aggressiveness is found in most of

Carroll's writings and derives from his jealousy of his sisters who displaced him from his mother's physical and emotional affections: "The wish to eat up and the fear of being eaten up are written over and over again in his fantasies, and appear on nearly every page of *Wonderland*."[14] Miss Greenacre does not mention "Brother and Sister," but it is a classic illustration of sibling rivalry. The psychoanalytical approach, which uses the poetry to confirm assumptions about the emotional make up of its author, has limited literary value; but it nevertheless highlights some of the more interesting facets of Carroll's personality.

Between 1855 and 1862 while at Oxford Carroll compiled a scrapbook called *Mischmasch*. One of the more interesting nonsense poems that appeared in that volume is "The Two Brothers"[15] (1853), a work which not only embodies the theme of sibling rivalry and oral aggressiveness, but cleverly plays with language. The poem, crudely illustrated by Carroll, is about two brothers who, upon leaving Twyford school, decide to go fishing. When they get to the bridge, the older brother joins his fishing rod together and "then a great hook he took from his book, / And ran it right into his brother." The unexpectedness of this violence, coupled with the sing-song effect produced by the meter and internal rhyme, creates a scene of comic grotesquerie unequalled since the *Ingoldsby Legends*. After he hurls his brother into the water the fish come to devour him, "for the lad that he flung was so tender and young, / It gave them an appetite." The younger brother asks, "What have I done that you think it such fun / To indulge in the pleasure of slaughter." The response is a series of joking puns:

> I am sure that our state's very nearly alike
> (Not considering the question of slaughter),
> For I have my perch on the top of the bridge,
> And you have your perch in the water.
> I stick to my perch and your perch sticks to you,
> We are really extremely alike;
> I've a turn-pike up here, and I very much fear
> You may soon have a turn with a pike.

Suddenly language and the delight in punning displace the "real world" of the baited brother. But then, there has never really been a real world to begin with. The older brother, despite his hostility, is a wit, a comic character, and not a sadistic homicidal maniac. Similar to many of the creatures Alice meets in Wonderland, the older brother chooses to play with language at a moment which in the real world would demand anything but detachment and wit for its own sake; and such behavior, of course, in the real world would be deemed mad. In the universe of nonsense, however, as the Cheshire Cat observes, "we're all mad." "The Two Brothers" ends, as does much nonsense poetry, arbitrarily; for there is no point or thesis or resolution possible. The boys' sister appears, discovers that she has brothers on either end of the fishing pole; and the older brother jauntily exclaims, "I's mighty wicked, that I is!" and says that he is going off to sea and never coming back. The younger brother, not surprisingly, is almost totally forgotten, except for the final detached observation by the sister: "One of the two will be wet through and through, / And t'other'll be late for his tea!"

Mischmasch contains a number of poems that are significant in Carroll's development as a writer of nonsense, including "She's All My Fancy Painted Him," which formed the basis of the White Rabbit's "evidence" at the trial of the Knave of Hearts, and the first stanza (written in 1855) of what was to become "Jabberwocky." Because these two works are associated with the mature and successful Carroll it seems hard to account for the transition from "The Two Brothers" to "Jabberwocky." But the principles of nonsense can be found to be operating in both the early and later poetry. The question then arises, why is one nonsense poem more interesting or successful than another? An attempt to answer that question will be made later in this chapter in the discussion of Carroll's classic nonsense pieces.

"She's All My Fancy Painted Him" copies the first line of "Alice Gray," a sentimental song by William Mee that was popular at the time. The rest of the poem bears no resemblance to the song except in the alternating iambic tetrameter and trimeter lines. Martin Gardner suggests that the song may have appealed to Carroll because it tells of the unrequited love of a man for a girl named Alice.[16] The original song opens, "She's all my fancy painted her, / She's lovely, she's divine, / But her heart it is another's / She never can be mine."[17] Carroll's poem also begins with a sense of loss, but the confusing use of pronouns quickly blocks out any meaning: "She's all my fancy painted him / (I make no idle boast); / If he or you had lost a limb, / Which would have suffered most?"[18] By the end of the poem, the relationship between the "I," "he," "you," "she," "we," and "they" is totally obfuscated—and the secret, as Robert Frost says, sits in the middle and knows: "Don't let him know she liked them best, / For this must ever be / A secret, kept for all the rest, / Between yourself and me." Although Carroll made major revisions in his poem before using it in *Wonderland,* the essential sense unnecessary for a Wonderland trial was already pruned from the 1855 version.

"The Palace of Humbug" (1855),[19] which also appeared in *Mischmasch,* opens with a parody of Alfred Bunn's "I dreamt I dwelt in marble halls, / With vassals and serfs at my side" (from *Bohemian Girl*): "I dreamt I dwelt in marble halls, / And each damp thing that creeps and crawls / Went wobble-wobble on the walls." As in Tennyson's "The Palace of Art," there are decorations on the arras, only here the pictures are dreary and socially decadent: "the humbugs of the social sphere." While wandering through the palace the narrator suddenly has a vision of "two worn decrepit men, / The fictions of a lawyer's pen, / who never more might breathe again." The narrator urges the servants of the two fictitious men (Richard Roe and John Doe) to rouse themselves from woe by tales of evidence, suit, demurrer, and defense. The servant of John Doe bends over him and shouts "Law!" at which he smiled and faintly muttered "Sue!"—for "Her name was legal too." Dawn appears, a hurricane sweeps away the narrator's vision, and the speaker says that to this day his spirit crawls when he remembers "that horrid dream of marble halls!"

The opening tercet of this poem is so striking that the remainder of the verse is disappointing. Here is a good example of a nonsense poem that does not engage the reader's interest beyond a few lines. It is too didactic, too many of the tercets make uninteresting sense, and the legal jokes are not very funny. The delicate balance between the real world (in this case, the law) and the world of nonsense, where words refer to other words, is lost—and the poem becomes silly. Perhaps Carroll was wise not to go beyond the first four lines of "Jabberwocky" in 1855.

Carroll's parody "The Three Voices"[20] adopts the meter and stanza form of Tennyson's "The Two Voices" and pokes fun at the grave, complex philosophical questioning of that sententious poem. The loudest of the three voices belongs to an old hag who relentlessly harasses the narrator with her umbrella and endless chatter: "She urged, 'No knife is like a fork,' / And ceaseless flowed her dreary talk." She is filled with pointless truisms: "The More exceeds the Less," "Each gives to more than each," and "Notion hath its source in Thought." The narrator is overwhelmed by her: "When he, with racked and whirling brain, / Feckly implored her to explain, / She simply said it all again." The narrator, like the poem, gets nowhere. Words and senseless rhetoric become ends in themselves, and the serious philosophic questions about the purpose of existence that Tennyson was seeking answers to are left far behind. Carroll's illustration of the hag with her umbrella sticking into the narrator's ribs makes abundantly clear that her silence will be dearly bought. Verbal oppression and nonsense are the two major thematic aspects of Carroll's verse that make it a parody.

"Upon the Lonely Moor,"[21] an early version of the White Knight's Ballad, which appeared in *The Train* in 1856, is a parody of Wordsworth's poem about the aged leech-gatherer, "Resolution and Independence." Carroll chose not to use the rhyme royal stanza of Wordsworth's poem but instead focussed upon the tone and subject matter of that work for his parody. The alternating tetrameter and trimeter provide a mocking quality in their relentless regularity: "I met an aged, aged man / Upon the lonely moor: / I knew I was a gentleman, / And he was but a boor." In his comic verse Carroll treats not only children with irreverence but also the aged. The hostility and violence of "The Two Brothers" has its counterpart here, in a refreshing anti-romantic and sadistic poem. Where Wordsworth reveres the simple honesty and stoical independence of the ancient leech-gatherer, Carroll torments his slightly mad old gentleman—who earns his living in such ways as by baking soap-bubbles into mutton pies which he sells in the street: "I did not hear a word he said, / But kicked that old man calm, / And said, 'Come, tell me how you live!' / And pinched him in the arm." The violence continues: "I gave his ear a sudden box, / And questioned him again, / And tweaked his grey and reverend locks, / And put him into pain." In an attempt to regularize the rhyme within each stanza Carroll changed several lines of this poem for the White Knight's song; and the hostility, though still present, is better controlled. Here are the revisions of the eight lines quoted above:

> So, having no reply to give
> To what the old man said,
> I cried "Come, tell me how you live!"
> And thumped him on the head.
> . . . .
> I shook him well from side to side
> Until his face was blue:
> "Come, tell me how you live," I cried,
> "And what it is you do!"[22]

The revisions are clearly superior in their economy and surprise—"And thumped him on the head" is a delightful non-sequitur enhanced by the funny word "thumped." The original lines are more violent, and consequently "put him into pain" is anti-climactic and unfunny padding to fill out the stanza.

Wordsworth ends "Resolution and Independence" with the narrator finding strength within himself gained by his remembering the leech-gatherer. The speaker in Carroll's poem concludes on a note of madness induced by his encounter with the absurd and eccentric old man:

> And now if e'er by chance I put
> My fingers into glue,
> Or madly squeeze a right-hand foot
> Into a left-hand shoe;
> Or if a statement I aver
> Of which I am not sure,
> I think of that strange wanderer
> Upon the lonely moor.

This poem makes no more sense than many of Carroll's earlier verses and yet it is more memorable. The fact that it parodies a well-known poem partially explains its effectiveness, for there is that pleasant tension between the sentimental original and the irreverent imitation. Furthermore, even taken by itself, the poem is comic. The unexplained hostility of the narrator toward the old man, when safely set forth in a jaunty rhythm and comic rhymes, becomes very funny. The fact that the speaker is less than sane himself (for he plans to keep the Menai bridge from rusting by boiling it in wine) enables him to behave towards the old man in the unconventional manner that he does. These early poems demonstrate a distinct move towards Wonderland, where all are mad, save Alice.

The best of Carroll's nonsense verse can be found in the two Alice books and in *The Hunting of the Snark*, the latter being his "Finnegans Wake." There is not enough time nor real call to discuss the many other pieces he wrote, such as *Phantasmagoria* (1869), a long poem about the antics of an unexperienced little ghost, "Hiawatha's Photographing" (the difficulties of a photographer set forth in the meter of "The Song of Hiawatha"), and numerous topical verses ("The Elections to the Hebdomadal Council," "The New Belfry of Christ Church, Oxford," etc.). The rest of this chapter, then, will focus upon the poems in *Alice's Adventures in Wonderland, Through the Looking Glass,* and *The Hunting of the Snark*.

b. The Poetry of Wonderland

Most of the poems in the two Alice books are parodies of poems or popular songs that were familiar to Carroll's contemporaries. The first to appear in *Alice's Adventures in Wonderland* is "How doth the little crocodile," a parody of Isaac Watts's moralistic little poem "Against Idleness and Mischief."[23] Watts uses the bee as an example of wholesome industriousness: "How skillfully she builds her cell! / And labours hard to store it well / With the sweet food she makes" (p. 39). Carroll's crocodile, on the other hand, does its work by remaining passive and merely opening its jaws: "How cheerfully he seems to grin, / How neatly spreads his claws, / And welcomes little fishes in, / With gently smiling jaws" (p. 38). Again, there is the theme of oral aggressiveness noted by Phyllis Greenacre, and· it is very aptly applied here. Watts's sentimental vision of the animal world is replaced by Carroll's Darwinian view of survival of the stronger. There is considerable pleasure to be derived from having such a cold picture of animal behavior, presented in the rhyme, meter, and near language of Watts's storybook view. Only the smile of the Cheshire Cat can exceed the sinister gentleness of the crocodile's smiling jaws. The very human—and non-Darwinian—attributes which Carroll gives to his predator suggest all too graphically the reality of social Darwinism. John Ciardi chooses to read this poem as a criticism of the hypocrisy in Watts's poem: "Is it too much to argue that the crocodile is a happy hypocrite piously gobbling up the trusting fishes (including the poor fishes among the readers who are willing to take Watts's prettily shallow morality as a true rule of life)?"[24]

Although shaped verse can be traced back to ancient Greece, Carroll's mouse's tale is one of the best known examples of the form. An earlier version, which appeared in *Alice's Adventures Undergound,* tells the story of some mice who were crushed beneath a mat by a dog and a cat that were pursuing a rat. The revision deals with a dog named Fury who suggests to a mouse that they both go to court, for "we must have a trial" (p. 51). The mouse protests that a trial without judge or jury would be meaningless, to which Fury responds: "I'll be judge, I'll be jury," and "I'll try the whole cause and condemn you to death." Unlike the original tale, the revision is absurd and violent. Fury wants a trial simply because "this morning I've nothing to do," and his view of justice is exceeded only by the Snark (which serves as judge, jury, and counsel for the defense). If this poem is a satire on the legal profession that aspect of it is incidental. It is primarily a piece of nonsense, a playing with language— seen in the shape of the poem and the punning introduction: "Mine is a long and sad tale!" said the Mouse. " 'It *is* a long tail, certainly,' said Alice, looking down with wonder at the Mouse's tail" (p. 50). The puns, the tail shape of the verse (like an illustration), Fury's lack of motivation (a dog not being the natural enemy of the mouse—whereas, in the early version, a mouse offers a good reason for disliking both cat and dog), and the non sequiturs are the essential aspects of the poem's nonsense. Its "statement," therefore, must be read in the context of Wonderland, where violence is usually verbal and impotent to harm the real world, represented by Alice.

In Wonderland Alice has difficulty in saying things as she remembered them. When she attempted to recite Watts's poem she spoke the parody. Now, at the request of the caterpillar, when she tries to repeat Robert Southey's "The Old Man's Comforts and How He Gained Them," she utters still another parody. As the Caterpillar later comments, her recital "is wrong from beginning to end." This poem is reminiscent of "Upon the Lonely Moor" in its unconventional treatment of old age. Southey's old man is incredibly smug about the comforts that his righteous behavior bestowed upon his age: "In the days of my youth I remember'd my God. / And He hath not forgotten my age" (p. 69). Carroll's old man is also proud of the youthful prowess he still retains, but is wonderfully short-tempered: " 'I have answered three questions, and that is enough,' " / Said his father. " 'Don't give yourself airs! / Do you think I can listen all day to such stuff? / Be off, or I'll kick you down stairs!' " (p. 71). Part of the humor of this conclusion comes from the old man's confusion of a literary convention with a personality—one does not expect him to take on the faceless speaker of the refrain "You are old, father William" because he is simply the conventional questioner who appears in the traditional ballad.

The lullaby which the Duchess sings to the pig-baby is a burlesque of G. W. Langford's "Speak Gently," which counsels that it is better to rule by love and gentleness than by fear: "Speak gently to the little child! / Its love be sure to gain; / Teach it in accents soft and mild; / It may not long remain" (p. 85). This saccharine advice is translated into that of comic violence and absurdity: "Speak roughly to your little boy, / And beat him when he sneezes: / He only does it to annoy, / Because he knows it teases" (p. 85). In some of the poems previously examined there was no explanation for why the characters behaved the way they did. Here the Duchess's advice is predicated upon the motive of a child teasing its parents, as if he could control his sneezing in a room full of pepper. When one expects motivation in Wonderland, it is not given; and when one does not expect it, it is made explicit. The poem intensifies the nonsense of Wonderland even when one does not know Langford's poem. When one thinks of the image of childhood presented by the nineteenth-century authors, Carroll's parody seems all the more refreshing and innovative.

Jane Taylor's well-known poem "The Star" is parodied in the Mad Hatter's song: "Twinkle, twinkle, little bat! / How I wonder what you're at! / Up above the world you fly, / Like a tea-tray in the sky. / Twinkle, twinkle—" (pp. 98–99). Elizabeth Sewell has analyzed the process by which Carroll turned the original four lines ("Twinkle, twinkle, little star, / How I wonder what you are!? / Up above the world so high, / Like a diamond in the sky!") into nonsense by attempting to answer why bats and tea-trays are more suitable to nonsense than are stars and diamonds:

A star is something exceedingly remote and beyond control; it has no apparent parts and can be assigned by the ordinary observer no definite qualities other than those of size and degree of brightness; it is beautiful . . . ; it is one of an unnumbered multitude. A bat is something near at hand, reasonably familiar, small; it is a creature whose appearance and habits are familiar; it is grotesque and we feel no attraction toward it; it usually appears alone. The other substitution, that of a tea-tray for a diamond, works on much the same principles, abandoning beauty, rarity, preciousness and attraction for ordinariness. It adds one further distinction, for a tea-tray is the work of man. In other words, the artificial is here preferred to the work of nature. Smallness, ordinariness, artificiality, distinctness of units, and a tendency to concentrate on the part rather than the whole are all helpful in the playing of Nonsense.[25]

One very important element which Sewell omits is the surprise that comes with the substitutions. Because we know the original poem the appearance of a bat startles us. Even without knowing the original, however, the bat is surprising because the two "twinkles" are totally inappropriate verbs to describe the actions of a bat. Furthermore, as Sewell does point out, the reader is unable to fuse together the image of the bat with the tea-tray, thereby keeping the two images discrete. One's imagination can, on the other hand, fuse stars and diamonds without any difficulty.

The Mock Turtle's song parodies the first line and employs the meter of Mary Howitt's poem "The Spider and the Fly." The opening stanza of Howitt's version reads:

> "Will you walk into my parlour?" said
>   the spider to the fly.
> " 'Tis the prettiest little parlour that
>   ever you did spy.
> The way into my parlour is up a
>   winding stair,
> And I've got many curious things to
>   show when you are there."
> "Oh, no, no," said the little fly, "to
>   ask me is in vain,
> For who goes up your winding stair can
>   ne'er come down again." (p. 133)

The Mock Turtle sings very slowly and sadly:

> "Will you walk a little faster?" said a
>   whiting to a snail,
> "There's a porpoise close behind us,
>   and he's treading on my tail.
> See how eagerly the lobsters and the
>   turtles all advance!
> They are waiting on the shingle—will
>   you come and join the dance?
> Will you, won't you, will you, won't you,
>   will you join the dance?
> Will you, won't you, will you, won't you,
>   won't you join the dance?" (p. 134)

The Mock Turtle, living up to its name, appears to be mocking here the moral of Howitt's poem. There is clearly no lesson to be learned from the song. Rather, it is an invitation to play, to dance. The rollicking rhythm of Howitt's poem is retained for its energetic playfulness, but the intrusive moral lesson has been left out of Wonderland. The whiting, the lobsters, and the snail, unlike the fly of Howitt's verse, have nothing to fear—for although they will be thrown out to sea, the experience will be "delightful" and, furthermore, as the whiting explains, if they are then far from England, they will be closer to France.

It would be wrong to take this as anti-Gallic sentiment. It is a statement of simple optimism—all that is and will be is right. The whiting concludes by exhorting the "beloved snail" to enter in the excitement of the dance, that is, into the amoral world of play. Donald Rackin has this further point: "Note how the Mock Turtle's song that accompanies the Lobster Quadrille twists the sadistic original . . . into an innocuous nursery rhyme. This parody demonstrates that Wonderland refuses to be consistent to itself: if the above-ground rhymes tend to hide or deny Darwinian theory, Wonderland's poems will be vengefully Darwinian; but if above ground rhymes admit the cruelty of nature, then Wonderland produces harmless nonsense verses."[26]

When Alice attempts to recite another moralistic poem by Watts, "The Sluggard," she again distorts it into an amoral, cruel, Darwinian commentary on nature. While Watts's poem preaches the gospel of hard work, Carroll's parody tells of a panther who "shares" a meat pie with an owl. The panther gets the meat pie and allows the owl to have the dish and the spoon. Then "the Panther received knife and fork with a growl. / And concluded the banquet by—." (p. 140). The grim final words, "eating the owl," appear in the 1886 printed edition of Savile Clarke's operetta. This poem not only makes fun of the self-righteousness of Watts's verse but comically subverts the sentimental picture of animal (and human?) behavior that characterized so much of children's literature in the Victorian era. An angry Vicar in Essex actually wrote a letter to *The St. James' Gazette* accusing Carroll of irreverence because of the Biblical allusion in the first line of his parody.[27] Such an attack is surprising, since Carroll's line " 'Tis the voice of the Lobster," is practically the same as Watts's " 'Tis the voice of the sluggard."

The Mock Turtle's mawkish song about beautiful soup is, of course, an appropriate commentary upon his own destiny and, like the poem Alice just finished reciting, depends upon oral aggressiveness for some of its humor. "Turtle Soup" is a parody of the popular song "Star of the Evening," by James Sayles, which opens,

> Beautiful star in heav'n so bright,
> Softly falls thy silv'ry light,

> As thou movest from earth afar,
> Star of the evening, beautiful star.
> Chorus:
> Beautiful star,
> Beautiful star,
> Star of the evening, beautiful star. (p. 141)

The Mock Turtle, in "a voice choked with sobs," begins: "Beautiful soup, so rich and green, / Waiting in a hot tureen! / Who for such dainties would not stoop? / Soup of the evening, beautiful Soup! / Soup of the evening, beautiful Soup!" (p. 141). The substitution of "soup" for "star" turns the parody into nonsense. A romantic apostrophe to a star, suggestive of beauty, aloofness, and purity is fairly conventional. But soup is not usually thought of as beautiful and an exclamatory song of praise for such a common food turns the parody into good nonsense.

The response of a Victorian reader to these poems from Wonderland would, of course, be very different from that of a twentieth-century reader. The poems that are parodied were familiar if not known by heart, to Carroll's contemporaries. The recognizable meter, imagery, and morals of these works had an *immediate* effect upon them. Carroll's poetry, furthermore, asserted a daring challenge to conventional, didactic children's poetry and satirized Victorian morality. The Victorians took seriously the familiar poetry of Watts, Southey, Langford, Taylor, Howitt, and Sayles. These respectable poets appeared in all the popular readers and, until Carroll, no one had reason to question their sanctity. A modern reader, on the other hand, is likely to be ignorant of the original poems. Nevertheless, Carroll's parodies survive and continue to delight. In their absurdity they have generated new meanings that no longer depend upon the verses that are parodied.

c. The Poetry of Looking-Glass Land

The first poem to appear in *Through the Looking Glass* is "Jabberwocky," perhaps the best known and most frequently discussed of all of Carroll's poetry. Martin Gardner draws an interesting analogy between it and abstract painting:

The realistic artist is forced to copy nature, imposing on the copy as much as he can in the way of pleasing forms and colors; but the abstract artist is free to romp with the paint as much as he pleases. In similar fashion the nonsense poet does not have to search for ingenious ways of combining pattern and sense—he takes care of the sounds and allows the sense to take care of itself. The words he uses may suggest vague meanings, like an eye here and a foot there in a Picasso abstraction, or they may have no meaning at all—just a play of pleasant sounds like the play of non-objective colors on a canvas.[28]

Characteristically, most of the nonsense words are nouns or adjectives. Carroll apparently wanted his sentences to look genuine (nouns, verbs, and predicates are usually easy to detect) so that he could avoid mere gibberish. Elizabeth Sewell offers an explanation as to why most of the verbs are not nonsense words: "In logic, a verb expresses a relation, and this suggests two reasons for the few invented verbs in Nonsense. The first is the impossibility of inventing new relations in logic. The second is that a verb is an expressed relation, and relations in logic have to be simple and exact."[29] Sewell does not accept on face value Humpty Dumpty's explanation of the words in "Jabberwocky" as portmanteaus: "*frumious*, for instance, is not a word, and does not have two meanings packed up in it; it is a group of letters without any meaning at all . . . it looks like other words, and almost certainly more than two."[30] The mind will play with a nonsense word and perhaps associate with it several genuine words, but as Carroll says, "if you have that rarest of gifts, a perfectly balanced mind, you will say 'frumious.' " Sewell goes on to comment that "the mind is encouraged by means of these Nonsense words to notice likenesses; but the likenesses are to other *words*. It is the purely verbal memory and associative faculty which is called into play."[31] The likenesses between images, however, are not perceived in nonsense; and the mind cannot fuse the verbal similarities together into a poetic unity.

There is, nevertheless, formal unity in "Jabberwocky," inasmuch as it is a mock-heroic ballad about an encounter between a young man and an adversary and appears to have a beginning, a middle, and an end (although the last stanza repeats the first). The young man, after being warned by his father of the Jabberwock, the Jubjub bird, and the Bandersnatch, goes off to do battle, slays the Jabberwock, and victoriously returns to his approving father. The conventional ballad stanza, the clear story line, the traditional syntax, and the many common words all provide a sensible framework of reference. The element of nonsense is restricted to the use of certain neologisms strategically placed in each stanza. If pure nonsense is conceived of as a field of closed language which resists an interpretation based upon some other system (e.g., ordinary prose, allegory, symbolism, etc.), then "Jabberwocky" is not pure nonsense. There are not enough "structures of resistance," as Michael Holquist calls them,[32] to close out of the poem ordinary meaning—in the battle between sense and nonsense, sense wins out in "Jabberwocky," despite the structures of resistance provided by the nonsense words.

Nevertheless, the central interest in "Jabberwocky" is not in its story line but in its language. Our unfamiliarity with "slithy toves," "borogoves," and "Bandersnatch" makes the poem fun. The words conjure up associations in our minds that provide a "feeling" for their meanings. The word "galumphing" illustrates the failure of pure nonsense. In the sentence "He left it dead, and with its head / He went galumphing back," the syntax makes it clear that "galumphing" describes how he went back. As the only nonsense word in an otherwise perfectly conventional sentence, the tendency of the mind is to break sense out of the word (and not to take it as a collection of letters that only has meaning in the context of the work). Consequently, associated words like "galloping" and "triumphantly" arise to help make sense of the sentence. One may, of course, come to accept "galumphing" as a word on its own, one that suggests a triumphant awkward gallop. If another reader makes similar associations, then we could actually converse with that word and be mutually understood. A. L. Taylor, for example, writes that "the little St. George with his vorpal sword is made very attractive in Tenniel's drawing and could not possibly galumph."[33] Carroll's own interpretation of the nonsense words in the poem, though sometimes whimsical, contributes to the reader's impulse to explain and understand them.

In the final analysis, the poem is a work to have fun with. Martin Gardner in his *The Annotated Alice* has enumerated the various explanations of the nonsense words and notes that eight of them reappear in *The Hunting of the Snark*. Some readers, such as A. L. Taylor, insist upon interpreting the poem.[34] He argues that Carroll is satirizing the religious controversies around him, and sees the Tum-tum tree as "certainly the Thirty-nine Articles which people like Jowett signed, according to Dodgson, for the sake of their bread and butter." The Jubjub bird and the Bandersnatch he explains as the Catholic and Protestant aspects of the English Church. "Vorpal" is a concoction of "verbal" and "Gospel." And the repetition of the first stanza at the end signifies that nothing has really changed, that one controversy (the Jabberwock) has been slain but the "outgribing" is as strident as ever. The difficulty with making an allegory out of the poem, as Taylor has done, is that it is arbitrary, unconvincing, and limits the interest of the poem if we stop with that reading. The poem has survived and perhaps thrived on countless interpretations of that variety. What the poem finally "means," of course, will never be settled, for it is not a secret language to be eventually decoded but a playful battle between sense and nonsense that can never be completely resolved into simple prose sense. As Alice says, after reading the poem, " 'Somehow it seems to fill my head with ideas—only I don't exactly know what they are! However, *somebody* killed *something*; that's clear, at any rate.—' "[35] Perhaps with Alice's response, the poem should be left at that.

Tweedledee's poem, "The Walrus and the Carpenter," satirizes the style of Thomas Hood's *Dream of Eugene Aram*. When Carroll gave the manuscript of his poem to Tenniel for illustrating, he offered the artist a choice of drawing a carpenter, butterfly, or baronet. Tenniel chose the carpenter. Any of the words would have suited the meter and rhyme scheme, and Carroll apparently had no strong preference as far as the nonsense was concerned. Since words in a nonsense poem are interchangeable, one would be well advised not to press such a poem too hard for a meaning. A butterfly or a baronet would serve equally well as a contrasting member of the pair walking near at hand along the beach. The nonsense would be less

effective, however, if the walrus were walking with a seal or
the carpenter with an electrician.

The opening stanza sets the tone for the absurdities to follow:

> The sun was shining on the sea,
> Shining with all his might:
> He did his very best to make
> The billows smooth and bright—
> And this was very odd, because it was
> The middle of the night. (p. 233)

The nonsense of such "darkness visible" is reinforced by the
rhyming of "bright" and "night" and the matter-of-fact regularity
of the meter. The Walrus and the Carpenter are as mad as any
of the creatures in Wonderland or Looking-Glass Land. They say
and do things without the logic of motivation and transition.
The Walrus, for example, after speculating whether seven
maids with seven mops could sweep away all the sand on the
beach in a half year, beseeches the oysters: "O oysters, come and
walk with us!" After the oysters, who wear shoes even though
they have no feet, follow the odd couple down the beach aways,
the Walrus speaks his famous stanza:

> "The time has come," the Walrus said,
> "To talk of many things:
> Of shoes—and ships—and sealing wax—
> Of cabbages—and kings—
> And why the sea is boiling hot—
> And whether pigs have wings." (p. 235)

The alliteration in the third and fourth lines and the rhyming
of "things," "kings," and "wings" suggest an affinity between
the words that does not, in fact, exist. "Shoes," "ships," "sealing-
wax," "cabbages," and "kings" make up a list of discrete items
that can no more be fused together than can the items in a
shopping list for a mad tea party. Nevertheless the whole stanza
has come to have a meaning almost independent of the poem—
namely, that the time has come to get down to essentials and
certainties. (In *The Adventures of Ellery Queen*, for example,
the first four lines of the stanza are an important factor in the

detective's method of frightening a confession out of a murderer).[36] This meaning probably derives from the fact that the Walrus's statement is a chronological, though non-logical, prelude to the eating of the oysters.

The theme of oral aggressiveness reappears in that the Walrus and Carpenter eventually devour all of the personified oysters. The Carpenter is ruthless and the Walrus sentimental, but the fact remains that they both ate the oysters. Alice likes the Walrus best for he was "a *little* sorry for the poor oysters." But Tweedledum then tells her that he ate as many as he could get, leaving Alice to conclude that "they were *both* very unpleasant characters."[37] This poem resembles Mary Howitt's sadistic verse "The Spider and the Fly" in its delicate, playful and fatal seduction of innocent, humanized creatures. The poem surpasses Darwinian vengefulness or "Nature red in tooth and claw," in that Carroll's creatures are humanized, and consequently their cruelty and indifference become monstrous. Still, like Alice, we do not judge them any more harshly than the phrase "very unpleasant" allows. They exist only in the nonsense world of Looking-Glass Land and are, in fact, further removed from Alice (and us) by having their existence in a poem recited by a Looking-Glass character. Cruelty and sadism, no matter how violent in Carroll's writings, are always carefully controlled and tempered.

After Humpty Dumpty explains away the mystery (and fun) of "Jabberwocky," he recites for Alice "In winter, when the fields are white" (p. 273), a poem, he tells her that "was written entirely for your amusement." The trouble is that the poem leaves Alice more puzzled than amused. The narrator of the poem sends a message to the fish: "This is what I wish." They reply: "We cannot do it, Sir, because—" (p. 274). At this point Alice remarks that she does not understand, and Humpty Dumpty assures her that it gets easier further on. The narrator urges the fish to obey his previous order and when they refuse he fills a kettle with water. Someone comes and tells him that the fish are in bed. The speaker screams into his ear, "Then you must wake them up again" (p. 275). Getting nowhere with this messenger, the narrator takes a corkscrew and goes to wake them up himself. He finds the door closed, and the last line of the poem reads, "I tried to turn the handle, but—" (p. 275). Alice asks if that is all, to which Humpty Dumpty replies, "That's all," and "Good-bye." Alice's relationship with Humpty Dumpty ends as abruptly as his poem.

This has to be the worst poem in the Alice books. The language is flat and prosaic, the frustrated story line is without interest, the couplets are uninspired and fail to surprise or to delight, and there are almost no true elements of nonsense present, other than in the unstated wish of the narrator and the lack of a conclusion to the work. But the poem's failure is important for what it reveals about Humpty Dumpty. He is the solemn literary man, the self-appointed critic of language who, though capable of a studious, self-assured explication of hard poems, cannot come up with a successful poem himself.

The last comic poem in *Through the Looking-Glass* is a riddle:

> "First, the fish must be caught."
> That is easy: a baby, I think, could have caught it.
> "Next, the fish must be bought,"
> That is easy: a penny, I think, would have bought it.
> "Now cook me the fish!"
> That is easy, and will not take more than a minute.
> "Let it lie in a dish!"
> That is easy, because it already is in it.
> "Bring it here! Let me sup!"
> It is easy to set such a dish on the table.
> "Take the dish-cover up!"
> Ah, *that* is so hard that I fear I'm unable!
> For it holds it like glue—
> Holds the lid to the dish, while it lies in the middle:
> Which is easiest to do,
> Un-dish-cover the fish, or dishcover the riddle?
>
> (p. 333)

Commenting on the riddle, why is a Raven like a writing desk, Elizabeth Sewell argues that "it is essential for Nonsense that the riddle should have no solution. It is propounded to keep the dream and disorder side of the mind in play, but there must be no answer which could set up some kind of unity between the parts."[38] Her point is well taken and may be applied to the White Queen's fish riddle. A solution would tie the verse together and make sense of it. Perhaps Carroll had no solution in mind but Martin Gardner offers a solution arrived at by a man named Peter Suckling: an oyster.[39] A baby can pick it from an oyster bed, a penny would buy one in Carroll's day, it cooks quickly, it lies in its own dish, it is easily placed on the table, but the "dish-cover" is hard to raise because it is held to the dish by the oyster in the middle. This solution makes perfectly good sense; and one could certainly argue that in Sewell's terms the verse is definitely not nonsense, but simply a conventional riddle. The solution, however, is not important in Looking-Glass Land, for after the White Queen finishes her recitation the Red Queen says to Alice, "Take a minute to think about it, and then guess"; but she then goes on to drink Alice's health and no opportunity is provided for Alice's response.

d.   The Hunting of the Snark

On July 18, 1874, Carroll went out for a walk in Guildford, the town where his sisters lived, and received the inspiration for his odyssey of nonsense, *The Hunting of the Snark*:

> I was walking on a hillside, alone, one bright summer day, when suddenly there came into my head one line of verse—one solitary line—"For the Snark *was* a Boojum, you see." I knew not what it meant, then: I know not what it means, now; but I wrote it down; and, sometime afterwards, the rest of the stanza occurred to me, that being its last line; and so by degrees, at odd moments during the next year or two, the rest of the poem pieced itself together, that being its last stanza.[40]

Carroll secured Henry Holiday, a prominent London painter and sculptor, to illustrate the poem, and his drawings successfully lived up to Carroll's desire that they be grotesque. The poem, which was published in March, 1876, received mixed reviews and at first did not sell many copies. Despite the fact that Carroll intended the book for children, it appealed mainly to adults. Sales began to pick up during the latter part of the century; by 1908 it had been reprinted seventeen times, and the many subsequent issues include several American editions. The following comment on the *Snark* by an anonymous reviewer in the *Athenaeum* for 1876 is typical of the bewilderment which the work generated:

It may be that the author of "Alice's Adventures in Wonderland" is still suffering from the attack of Claimant on the brain, which some time ago numbed or distracted so many intellects. Or it may be that he has merely been inspired by a wild desire to reduce to idiocy as many readers, and more especially, reviewers as possible. At all events, he has published what we may consider the most bewildering of modern poems.[41]

Many attempts have been made to read *The Hunting of the Snark* as an allegory. Carroll himself responded to the allegorist: "...I have received courteous letters from strangers, begging to know whether 'The Hunting of the Snark' is an allegory, or contains some hidden moral, or is a political satire: and for all such questions I have but one answer, '*I don't know!*'"[42] The allegorists continue into our own century. In 1911 Devereux Court argued that the poem satirizes an unsound business venture. Dean Donham, a former Dean of the Harvard School of Business Administration, said that the Boojum is a symbol of a business slump and the entire poem is a tragedy about the business cycle. Alexander Taylor reads the poem as an anti-vivisectionist tract. Martin Gardner sees it to be an existentialist treatise in which the Boojum is comparable to the atomic bomb.[43] Even W. H. Auden joins the allegorists in his suggestions that the ship can stand for mankind and human society moving through time and struggling with its destiny.[44]

The most interesting commentary on the poem to date is Michael Holquist's "What is a Boojum? Nonsense and Modernism."[45] Holquist's reading of the poem is strongly influenced by Elizabeth Sewell, as can be seen in his following comment:

Lewis Carroll's 'agony in eight fits' was not only among the first to exemplify what is perhaps the most distinctive feature of modern literature, it did so more openly, more paradigmatically than almost any other text one knew. That is, it best dramatized the attempt of an author to insure through the structure of his work that the work could be perceived only as what it was, and not some other thing;

the attempt to create an immaculate fiction, a fiction that resists the attempts of readers, and especially those readers who write criticism, to turn it into an allegory, a system equitable with already existing systems in the non-fictive world.[46]

Holquist argues that in the *Snark* Carroll achieves pure order, that by employing various "structures of resistance" he keeps the reader consistently off balance in any attempt he may make to draw "sense" from the poem. He cites six such structures of resistance which insure the poem's hermetic nature: 1. The acrostic dedicatory poem indicates that Carroll is more concerned with words that will exist in his own idiosyncratic system than in the conventional system of English; 2. the rule of three operates as a system for determining a truth that is absolutely unique to this poem and furthermore indicates that the intrinsic logic of the poem is not that of extrinsic logic which operates in systems outside the construct of the poem; 3. the various names of the crew members all begin with the letter *B*, a parallel that is rigidly observed, which dramatizes itself, but only as a dynamic process of parallelism, and nothing else; 4. the Butcher's proof that two can be added to one sets up an equation that is a process which begins with no content and ends with no content—it is pure process which has no other end than itself, namely the number 3; 5. the portmanteau words create new meanings (unique to the poem) by philologically exploiting the divergence between two old meanings; 6. the rhyme binds together words through their similar sounds, but no associative meaning links them and no resultant new association is possible.[47]

Holquist finally asks, "if *The Hunting of the Snark* is an absolute metaphor, if it means only itself, why read it?" He states that there are several answers, but chooses only to give one, "that it may help us to understand other, more complex attempts to do the same thing in modern literature."[48] It seems ironic for him to have argued so well that the *Snark* is an autonomous fiction and then to conclude that the reason one ought to read it is to better understand *other* autonomous fictions, like Franz Kafka's and Vladimir Nabokov's. A much sounder reason for reading the *Snark* is that it is enjoyable in and of itself. One does not read Virginia Woolf to understand William Faulkner—so why should one read Carroll simply to understand Kafka? The *Snark* is like an elaborate literary enigma which one need not feel compelled to solve in order to enjoy. It is a poem that one must relax into with no expectations other than to enjoy the process of a voyage through a unique world constructed solely out of words. If one glimpses occasional "meanings" or recognizes occasional familiar landmarks those are simply door prizes of the adventure.

The Hunting of the Snark is a mad adventure story cast in the form of a ballad. A crew, comprised of a Bellman, a Baker, a Barrister, a Billiard-marker, a Banker, a Bonnetmaker, a Broker, a Boots, a Butcher, and a Beaver, set out to hunt a Snark. The Bellman is captain of the ship and the person who organized the Snark hunt. The poem focuses, however, more intensely upon the Baker than upon any other single character. Carroll describes him at great length in the opening fit. He was famed for the number of items he forgot when he entered the ship; his umbrella, watch, jewels, rings, clothes, and, worse of all, his name. He is wearing, however, seven coats and three pairs of boots. He has a small intellect but his courage is perfect and as the Bellman noted, "is the thing that one needs with a Snark."

The ocean map that the Bellman provides for the crew is an absolute blank. His only plan for crossing the ocean is to tinkle his bell. In a more practical vein, he cites to his crew the five unmistakable characteristics of a snark: 1. its taste is hollow but crisp, 2. it habitually rises late, 3. it is slow in taking a jest, 4. it is fond of bathing-machines, 5. it is ambitious. Then he makes this all important distinction: "For, although common Snarks do no manner of harm, / Yet, I feel it my duty to say, / Some are Boojums—The Bellman broke off in alarm, / For the Baker had fainted away."[49] The Baker explains his seizure by citing his uncle's advice concerning the capture of a snark:

> "You may seek it with thimbles—and seek it with care;
> You may hunt it with forks and hope;
> You may threaten its life with a railway-share;
> You may charm it with smiles and soap—"
> . . . .
> "But oh, beamish nephew, beware of the day,
> If your Snark be a Boojum! For then

You will softly and suddenly vanish away,
And never be met with again!" (p. 56)

In the climactic Fit the Eighth, the warning of the Baker's
uncle is realized. The crew discover the Baker, "their hero,"

Erect and sublime, for one moment of time.
In the next, that wild figure they saw
(As if stung by a spasm) plunge into a chasm,
While they waited and listened in awe.

"It's a Snark!" was the sound that first came to their ears,
And seemed almost too good to be true.
Then followed a torrent of laughter and cheers:
Then the ominous words, "It's a Boo—"

Then silence. Some fancied they heard in the air
A weary and wandering sigh
That sounded like "—jum!" but the others declare
It was only a breeze that went by. (pp. 86–87)

The crew searches in vain for any trace of the Baker's body
and the poem closes with the lines, "He had softly and suddenly vanished away— / For the Snark *was* a Boojum, you see"
(p. 89). Holiday's illustration of the scene shows the Bellman's hand ringing his bell for the passing of the Baker. If one
looks carefully into the central darkness of the drawing he
will see the huge head of the Baker, terror on his face, and a
gigantic beak or claw pulling him by the wrist into total darkness.
    Perhaps Holquist is correct in arguing that the poem is self-
contained, but the paraphrasable aspects of the search for the
Snark and its consequences for the Baker have elicited two interesting commentaries. Martin Gardner suggests that the strongest
motif in the poem is "the dread, the agonizing dread, of ultimate failure. The Boojum is more than death. It is the end of all
searching. It is the final, absolute extinction."[50] This reading
is reinforced by Phyllis Greenacre's observation that central to
Carroll's life and writing is a voyeuristic theme. In the *Snark*
the penalty for looking is the disappearance of the spectator.
She says that "the most constant punitive threat" in his writings
"is of extinction, either by disappearance of the whole body

or by decapitation."[51] Although it is impossible to establish a coherent allegorical reading of the poem, it does seem possible to go beyond the limits that Holquist sets down for the poem—namely, the poem itself. Despite the "structures of resistance" Carroll does use words, phrases, and structures that permeate the shabby, disordered world of reality. There is, in fact, expressed in this poem anxiety over the threat of annihilation, and the Baker does, indeed, vanish. One does not, however, have to go as far as Gardner and argue that the poem is existential. There are simply too many details and characters which have nothing to do with existentialism. It even sounds foolish to speak of the Baker as having existential anguish. His character is too absurd and unreal to accommodate such philosophical gear. Still, the motif of dreading annihilation is a major aspect of the poem; and since this anxiety co-exists outside of the poem, one's response to the Baker's fate is necessarily conditioned by non-poetic circumstances. Such human responses to the poem are not all resisted—and they provide the glimpses of occasional "meaning" and the occasional familiar landmarks without which nonsense would revert to gibberish. "Pure order" may exist in mathematics but not in the world of words. Francis Bacon knew and complained of this in his comments on the Idols of the Market-Place.

Perhaps the best spirit to adopt when reading the poem is the one exemplified in Gardner's explanation of the Snark's five unmistakable marks: "The forks are for eating crisp Snark meat. The railway share appeals to the Snark's ambition to become wealthy and so can be used for baiting a death trap. Smiles are to let the Snark know when a pun has been perpetrated. The soap is of course for the bathing machines that the Snark carries about, and the thimble is used for thumping the side of the creature's head to wake him in time for five-o'clock tea."[52] Finally, it should be pointed out that a Boojum is not simply a Boojum. The dominant letter *B* closely associates the otherwise disparate crew. When a Snark is a Boojum, it, too, is brought under the umbrella of the *B*. The emphasis upon *was* in the line "For the Snark *was* a Boojum, you see" suggests that it was a Boojum all along, and the recognition of that fact proved to be an alliterative fatality.

CHAPTER 4

Alice

I   Alice's Adventures in Wonderland

ALTHOUGH Lewis Carroll wrote *Alice's Adventures in Wonderland* explicitly to entertain children, it has become the treasure of philosophers, literary critics, biographers, clergymen, psychoanalysts, and linguists, not to mention mathematicians, theologians, and logicians. There appears to be something in *Alice* for everyone, and there are almost as many explanations of the work as there are commentators. It is helpful for the reader to know, for example, about Carroll's linguistic playfulness, his mathematical and logic puzzles, his religious opinions, his nostalgia for childhood and preoccupation with death. Finally, however, the ideal reader would be one who could maintain a balance of the various critical approaches to *Alice*. Derek Hudson, perhaps the most sensible writer on Carroll, reminds us that Carroll was primarily a humorist: "The nearest parallel to the humorous method of Lewis Carroll is probably that of the Marx Brothers, whose dialogue not only has many verbal similarities with his but who also, like him, assert one grand false proposition at the outset and so persuade their audiences to accept anything as possible." Hudson goes on to note that it would be as foolish to look for sustained satire in the one as in the other: "Both have been based largely on a play with words, mixed with judicious slapstick, and set within the framework of an idiosyncratic view of the human situation; their purpose is entertainment."[1]

In Wonderland all things are possible. It is called Wonderland because, like Alice, the reader is continually astonished, surprised and puzzled. It is a world made up of contradictions, violence, jokes, anxiety, puns, puzzles, rudeness, rules and anarchy shaped by a dream vision. The chaos that rules in Won-

derland is not unfamiliar to us. It is evident in the humor of
the Marx Brothers and in the behavior of children who have
not yet been permeated with the rules of decorum. Little
Leroy's throwing his cereal at W. C. Fields and Chico Marx's
insulting a fat, wealthy lawyer are not unlike the behavior of
the Mad Hatter at the tea party. The misconduct of a child is
more easily taken for granted—but witness that same behavior
in an adult and he will be labelled either abnormal, mad, or
comic, depending upon the circumstances. In Wonderland everyone is mad, as the Cheshire Cat points out, and yet they are
all comic. Alice is faced with a world of adults who behave like
children, despite the variety of intellectual sophistication they
represent.

Alice's Adventures is a work of nonsense and as such lacks the
coherent structure of more conventional literary works. Although a dream vision is a conventional literary form that goes
back to the middle ages, Alice's dream differs from it in that it
is distinctly episodic, is rendered from the third person point
of view, and resists a coherent symbolic or allegorical interpretation. Alice's character does not appear to develop or sig-
nificantly change throughout the tale. One chapter does not
necessarily evolve out of the preceding one. The book sets forth
a series of discrete encounters between Alice and the creatures
in Wonderland, and she rarely seems capable of applying what
she learned in a past encounter to a new one and consequently
moves through her dream world in almost constant amazement.
Curiosity above all else impels Alice on to new adventures.

Many critics have attempted to explain *Alice's Adventures
in Wonderland*, to make sense of nonsense. One critic sees it
as a commentary upon contemporary ecclesiastical history;
another sees Alice as symbolic of the phallus, and her trip as a
reversion to her mother's womb, and still another sees it as an
existential commentary on meaning in a meaningless world. The
critics fall into several categories: biographical, psychoanalytical,
logical-linguistic, esthetic, Jungian, mythic, existential, socio-
logical, philosophical, theological, and literary comparatist. At
this juncture in Carroll criticism and scholarship, one would do
well to be eclectic and to reread the story in the light of the
various schools of criticism in so far as they clarify or enrich

the story—while recognizing that there is no single meaning to the adventures.

Let it be said at the outset that although the Alice books were originally intended for children—indeed, very specific ones—they have since been appropriated by adults. Most children today, if they know Alice at all, are familiar with the popular and sentimentalized versions of her presented in films and cartoons. The twentieth-century adult mind is very much at home in the violent, nightmarish dream world of the original Alice. The Victorians, however, had certain expectations of children's literature; and Carroll did not satisfy those expectations. As Elsie Leach has pointed out, few Victorian authors chose to model their stories upon the fairy tale or to embody elements of the fairy tale in their narratives for children. Hans Christian Anderson's fairy tales were translated into English by 1846, but no English writer had yet followed his practice. Carroll chose not to follow the established pattern of children's books, which demanded realism and moral didacticism, in favor of characteristics of the fairy tale. Elsie Leach observes that his tentative title, *Alice Among the Elves,* suggests that he recognized the fact himself. Although there are no elves in the book, there are magical transformations and changes in size, talking animals, and magical potions and foods. Furthermore, by choosing a dream structure for his work, Carroll rejects the approach of earlier writers in their appeal to the reason of the readers.

The character of Alice also departs from the conventional girl heroine. As Leach notes, the typical children's book presented "girl angels fated for an early death," or "impossibly virtuous little ladies," or "naughty girls who eventually reform in response to heavy adult pressure."[2] Alice is neither naughty or excessively nice, but curious and bewildered. She may grow up physically; but her experiences do not apparently teach her anything, alter her behavior, or prepare her for adulthood in a conventional way. Compared to the standard literature for children, *Alice* was surprisingly anti-didactic.

Whether playing railroad at Croft Rectory, working puzzles at Oxford, or telling stories to little girls, Carroll was intent on transforming his small corner of Victorian England into a rigorous and extraordinary adventure. After three short paragraphs

Alice is whisked off the humdrum surface of the earth and is plummeted into Wonderland. Like the other great adventurers of her time, Alice is strongly motivated by curiosity. At times she almost seems to be a disembodied intellect, so cool is she in the face of danger. While she is falling down the rabbit-hole, for instance, "she had plenty of time as she went down to look about her, and to wonder what was going to happen next."[3] As she continues her fall she rather casually removes from a passing shelf a jar of orange marmalade. To her disappointment it is empty and rather than drop it and risk hitting someone below, she places it in a cupboard as she falls past it.

Her composure is extraordinary (to think of food at a time like that)—and yet she has an intellectual appreciation of her fall, for she says that now "I shall think nothing of tumbling down stairs" (p. 27). The naïveté of her coolness, however, is quietly undermined by a joke the narrator makes about death: "'Why, I wouldn't say anything about it, even if I fell off the top of the house!' (which was very likely true)" (p. 23). One can see a connection in Carroll's mind betwen the death of childhood and the development of sex. This connection is also made at the end of the story where Alice is innocent of all knowledge of what the Knave of Hearts is likely to have been doing. The poem that introduces the Looking-Glass ("Come, hearken then, ere voice of dread, / With bitter summons laden, / Shall summon to unwelcome bed / A melancholy maiden") supports the sex-death relationship and elicits a comment by Empson: "After all the marriage-bed was more likely to be the end of the maiden than the grave, and the metaphor firmly implied treats them as identical."[4]

A great deal of the humor found in Alice's encounters with the creatures of Wonderland derives from the solemnity of Alice herself. She is almost totally lacking in a sense of humor; and the reader, along with the narrator, is always a step or two ahead of her. Alice is a kind of "straight man" not only to the inhabitants of Wonderland but to the author as well. More often than not the reader sees things through Alice's eyes, but Carroll's choice of third-person narrative gives one the perspective necessary for comedy.

Like Carroll working out mathematical puzzles when he was

falling asleep, Alice attempts to calculate how many miles she has fallen. Then her mind turns to Dinah, her cat; but she cannot imagine how to fit her into this strange new world, for there are no mice in the air. Again her mind reverts to abstractions as she wonders if cats eat bats or bats eat cats, until she finally starts dozing, only to be awakened by her sudden landing in Wonderland.

Although all the doors around the hall are locked Alice finds a tiny golden key which opens one that leads into a small passage. She kneels down and looks along the passage into "the loveliest garden you ever saw" (p. 30). Because of her size she is unable to get out of the dark hall to "wander among those beds of bright flowers and those cool fountains" (p. 30). It is not until Chapter VIII that Alice reaches the garden, only to discover that the roses are painted and the inhabitants either mad or cruel. The symbolism of the garden has elicited no less than two interpretations. One critic believes that "the story revolves about the golden key to the enchanted garden and Alice's endless frustrations and wanderings in bypaths until she enters at last," and that the garden is a "rich symbol if we call it adult life viewed by a child, or vice versa."[5] Another critic conjectures on the perspective of the adult: "As sublibrarian of Christ Church, Carroll used a small room overlooking the deanery garden when the Liddell children played croquet. How often he must have watched them, longing to escape from the dark halls of Oxford into the bright flowers, and cool fountains of childhood's Eden!"[6]

Alice is constantly at odds with the creatures and situations of Wonderland. It is precisely this tension between her expectations and the actuality of Wonderland that the book is all about. Alice is "our" representative in a world of disorder, contradiction, violence, arbitrariness, cruelty, rudeness, frustration, and amorality. Jan B. Gordon wonders "whether Alice's attempt during her *Adventures* to constitute a social family among the animals is not the burden of the Victorian exile."[7] He sees the character of Alice to be determined by the Victorians' equating the child with the adult, an action which has the unfortunate effect of creating an orphan. Donald Rackin sees Alice in more universal terms and calls the *Adventures* "a comic myth of man's insoluble problem of meaning in a meaningless world."[8] The only trouble with that summary is that it overlooks the playfulness of the work. The solemnity of the quotation might best be seen if it were applied to the Marx Brothers' *Duck Soup*, a movie which contains many of the characteristics of Wonderland.

The first thing Alice has to learn to control in Wonderland is her own body. By drinking from a mysterious bottle and eating from a small cake she experiences great changes in body size until she becomes unsure of her own identity: "Who in the world am I? Ah, that's the great puzzle" (p. 37). Throughout her adventures Alice is confronted with the problem of her shifting identity, a problem aggravated and in large part caused by the inconsistencies of Wonderland. As Rackin points out, "the nearly universal belief in permanent self-identity—is put to the test and eventually demolished in Wonderland."[9] Alice finally overcomes the threat to her selfhood at the conclusion of the story, when, having grown to her full size, she asserts "You're nothing but a pack of cards!" (p. 161). This capability for sudden changes in body size can be seen as an ominous and destructive process that undermines the above-ground validity of natural growth and predictable size. Through the destruction of stability, Wonderland asserts its mad sanity. The two other above-ground assumptions that are destroyed are the hierarchy of animals and men, and consistent identity.[10] The theme of maturation is also demonstrated here: "Children like to think of being so small that they could hide from grown-ups and so big that they could control them, and to do this dramatises the great topic of growing up, which both Alices keep to consistently."[11]

After vainly puzzling over her identity, Alice finds herself swimming in a pool of tears which she wept when she was nine feet tall. Carroll typically grants his heroine incredible powers of distraction. Alice not only thinks about marmalade instead of death but now worries about the proper way to address a mouse she finds swimming in her tears. The prospect of drowning does not enter her mind as she proceeds to engage the mouse in conversation. The image of the tears as a sea supplants in dream-like fashion the actual hall of tears—for the mouse and

Alice, joined as if by magic by birds and other animals, swim "to the shore."

A rather extreme, but interesting, interpretation of the pool of tears is provided by Empson: "The symbolic completeness of Alice's experience is I think important. She runs the whole gamut; she is a father in getting down the hole, a foetus at the bottom, and can only be born by becoming a mother and producing her own aminotic fluid."[12] Gordon, on the other hand, suggests a Victorian framework in which to read this section:

One of the first things Alice learns in Wonderland is that punishment for transgression, a constant fear in the topside existence, is just as much a threat to her in the new environment. But rather than crying at the prospect of receiving physical punishment from those who lay down the law, she comes to understand that one is punished to stop the distress of previous punishment, not for any literal sins. Her own tears have resulted in the deep pool in which she finds herself, and yet she fears the further chastisement of being drowned in her own tears. . . . Carroll is actually making an astute observation on Victorian education, notably that the aquisition of knowledge and guilt over assumed transgression often accompany each other in nineteenth-century theories of development.[13]

Alice's concern for the correct form of address to the mouse is a reminder that nonsense is a game of words, and Chapter III reinforces this aspect of the story. The mouse proposes to dry Alice and the other animals by relating to them a piece of dry history. When the mouse states that "Stigand, the patriotic archbishop of Canterbury, found it advisable" (p. 47), the Duck interrupts to ask what the antecedent of "it" is: "I know what 'it' means well enough, when I find a thing . . . it's generally a frog or a worm" (p. 47). Such analysis and questioning is obviously detrimental to communication; but since the mouse's purpose in relating this history is to dry off the fellow creatures, such an attack upon grammatical ambiguity is doubly absurd. The Dodo finally settles upon a caucus-race to dry everyone off. When Alice asks what kind of a race that is, the Dodo replies that "the best way to explain it is to do it" (p. 48), a remark that suggests the inadequacy of language to explain all things. After the race is run everybody is declared the winner and all are awarded prizes, which seems like a perfectly acceptable democratic arrangement considering that everyone has gotten dry. Like so many anxious children, the animals all crowd around Alice, calling out "Prizes! Prizes!" The Dodo solemnly awards Alice her own thimble, perhaps an emblem of her fated domesticity. The animals all take this absurd ceremony very seriously and cause Alice to look as solemn as she can. In Tenniel's illustration of the ceremony there is pictured in the background among the birds the face of an ape. Although never mentioned in the text, the ape is perhaps meant to be a grim reminder of Darwin's recent investigations.

Carroll may have intended the caucus-race to satirize the activities of political parties. As one critic suggests, Carroll might have been poking fun at "the fact that committee members generally do a lot of running around in circles, getting nowhere, and with everybody wanting a political plum."[14] This episode also has a biographical interest, for a number of the animals in this race appear to be based upon actual people. The Duck is Canon Robinson Duckworth; the Lory is Lorina Liddell; Edith is the Eaglet; and the Dodo is Carroll. When he stuttered in pronouncing his name it came out "Do-Do-Dodgson."

The Mouse's tale is still another instance of language as play. "Tale" is confused with "tail," "not" with "knot," and the shape of the verse depicts a tail in Alice's mind. When one thinks back on this chapter he realizes that despite all the dialogue Alice has learned very little from her associates and vice-versa. The strategy of Wonderland is to defeat logical communication, to keep details from culminating into some meaningful order. Consequently, the reader, not to mention Alice, cannot evaluate past experiences and can only look forward to new and more bizarre ones. In the case of the Mouse's tale, however, there is a faint foreshadowing of the trial at the end of the book. The law is an issue in both, and both the tale and the trial exhibit linguistic confusion.

Chapter IV is the weakest section of the *Adventures;* for it comes close to abandoning nonsense, the language of play, for ordinary discourse, as the White Rabbit attempts to remove Alice from his house. The texture of the chapter is thin; and it does not complicate or develop any of the earlier motifs, save that of Alice's confusion about her identity. As she grows large and fills the house she becomes uncomfortable and almost regrets that she went down the rabbit hole. Empson finds in this scene a nightmare theme of the birth-trauma: "she grows too big for the room and is almost crushed by it." He sees the theme repeated "more painfully after she seems to have got out; the rabbit sends her sternly into its house and some food there makes her grow again."[15] He also notes that in Carroll's drawing of Alice she is much more in the foetus position than she is in the Tenniel illustration. Empson apparently responds more dramatically to his claustrophobia than does Alice, whose curiosity and simple bewilderment are expressed in a remarkably detached tone: "it's rather curious, you know, this sort of life!" (p. 58). Her reality becomes a kind of fiction: "When I used to read fairy tales, I fancied that kind of thing never happened, and now here I am in the middle of one!" (p. 59).

Her thoughts are quickly interrupted as a crowd gathers outside the house. They rather sadistically force Bill the lizard down the chimney, but the problem of removing Alice is only resolved after Alice eats some magical cake and shrinks. The difficulties she experienced as a giant are now balanced by her encounter with an enormous puppy that threatens her life in its exuberant playfulness. Somehow a puppy seems out of place in Wonderland. It barks instead of speaks, it chases a stick, pants, and jumps in the air. It is all too much a creature from above ground and disfigures the character of Wonderland that has already been established. There is a little too much of second-rate *Gulliver's Travels* in this chapter to make it memorable; and one is happily relieved when Alice finally comes upon the mysterious large blue caterpillar quietly smoking a long hookah, for here. indeed, is Wonderland again.

Like so many of the creatures Alice meets, the Caterpillar treats her rudely, almost contemptuously. What makes this encounter unsettling is that the author provides absolutely no motivation for the Caterpillar's aggressiveness towards Alice. His insults are gratuitous, funny and intimidating. Alice, however, expects to be treated in the polite manner customary above ground. The Caterpillar's first question to her —"Who are *You?*"—

is not only contemptuous but especially unnerving considering Alice's previous difficulty in answering that question. It is almost as if the Caterpillar had read her anxieties and set this question to torment her. He does, after all, possess extra-sensory perception. As he gets down from the mushroom he tells her that eating one side will make her grow taller and the other side will make her grow shorter. " 'One side of *what*? The other side of *what*? thought Alice to herself. 'Of the mushroom,' said the Caterpillar, just as if she had asked it aloud" (p. 73).

After Alice repeats "You are old, Father William," the Caterpillar declares, "That is not said right." When Alice responds, "Not quite right, I'm afraid," he rejoinders—"It is wrong from beginning to end" (p. 72). He is, of course, correct inasmuch as the parody she uncontrollably recites undermines the whole character of Southey's poem. Furthermore, as Elizabeth Sewell points out, "Poetry is dangerous to Nonsense, even if unsatisfactory, even if parodied, and it is well to reduce it to criticism at once."[16] The Caterpillar is not only critical of Alice and her recitation, he is bored with her: "In a minute or two the Caterpillar took the hookah out of its mouth, and yawned once or twice, and shook itself. Then it got down off the mushroom, and crawled away into the grass" (p. 73). Alice is to be excused for nearly losing her temper with this creature—in fact she is to be praised for her remarkable equanimity in the face of an experience that might make anyone else feel psychotic.

The Pigeon, whom Alice meets next, continues to plague her with questions of identity. The Pigeon believes Alice is a serpent that is after her eggs. When she protests that she is not a serpent the Pigeon asks, "Well! *What* are you?" and the best that Alice can come up with is "I—I'm a little girl" (p. 76). But Alice's elongated neck suggests convincingly that she looks more serpentine than girlish to the Pigeon—and, furthermore, since girls as well as serpents eat eggs, it really makes no difference to the Pigeon, for then girls are a kind of serpent. Defining an entire creature by a single action has a particular logic from the Pigeon's point of view, and the newness of the idea silences Alice. The Caterpillar's and now the Pigeon's aggressive attack seriously threaten Alice's assumption of a permanent identity. Later, when the White Rabbit orders her about like his servant, Alice imagines that her new identity will surface in the world above when her cat Dinah will command her in the same manner. Empson goes behind the question of identity raised in this section to observe, "Alice knows several reasons why she should object to growing up, and does not at all like being an obvious angel, a head out of contact with its body that has to come down from the sky, and gets mistaken for the Paradisal serpent of the knowledge of good and evil, and by the pigeon of the Anunciation, too."[17]

The irrational behavior of the creatures in Wonderland is further developed in Chapter VI. The Footman sitting on the step of the Duchess' house takes for granted the chaos around him. When a plate flies out of the door and breaks against one of the trees behind him, he continues talking nonsense "exactly as if nothing had happened" (p. 81). Once inside, Alice meets the Duchess, one of the most unwholesome characters in the book. She is incredibly ugly, masculine, sadistic, moralistic, and sexually aggressive. The fact that she is first pictured nursing a baby makes her appear even more grotesque, for she is the antithesis of a maternal figure. The Cheshire Cat with it unnerving grin adds still another element of the grotesque to this caricature of domesticity. This is the home of chaos. There is pepper in the air and the cook is throwing everything within her reach at the Duchess and the baby. When Alice attempts to control the situation the Duchess quickly puts her in her place: "If everybody minded their own business the world would go round a deal faster than it does" (p. 84). And when Alice starts talking about the world spinning on its axis, the Duchess, by way of a pun, escalates the violence: "Talking of axis, chop off her head!" (p. 84). But her violence is aimless and quickly turns upon the baby: "she began nursing her child again, singing a sort of lullaby to it as she did so, and giving it a violent shake at the end of every line" (p. 85). She then proceeds to toss the baby violently up and down "and the poor little thing howled so" (p. 85) that Alice could hardly hear the words of the lullaby.

Alice is left to nurse the baby as the Duchess prepares to play croquet with the Queen. The extended parody of motherhood is finally terminated when the baby turns into a pig. Alice thinks to herself, "If it had grown up it would have made a dreadfully

ugly child: but it makes rather a handsome pig, I think" (p. 87).
Here again is another reminder that in Wonderland the essence
of anything is unstable. There are no rules, no conventions, no
categories—the comedy of chaos reigns supreme. And Alice's subsequent conversation with the Cheshire Cat takes her a step
further into the confusion.

Cats are not in the habit of sitting in trees or grinning, yet
the Cheshire Cat does both. Its very long claws and great many
teeth further contribute to the uneasiness and respect with which
Alice greets the creature. In a world devoid of structure Alice
rather naturally asks directions: "Would you tell me, please,
which way I ought to go from here?" The Cat replies, "That
depends a good deal on where you want to get to." When Alice
hesitates with "I don't much care where—" the Cat quickly
interrupts, "Then it doesn't matter which way you go." Alice
goes on to complete her remark saying "—so long as I get *somewhere*"(p. 88) but one surmises that Wonderland has already
spoken in its usual existential-like tones. Alice seemingly cannot
escape the madness of chaos that surrounds her. She protests that
she does not want to go among mad people, but the Cat know-
ingly replies, "we're all mad here. I'm mad. You're mad" (p. 89).
Although the reader may feel that Alice is the only vestige of
sanity in the book, from the Cat's point of view Alice's curiosity
and expectations may appear quite mad. Alice, in any case, does
not believe that her coming to Wonderland proves her mad. She
never comprehends the Cat's revelations about this disordered
world and persists in her subsequent adventures to expect conventional behavior from the mad inhabitants.

In her Jungian reading of the story, Judith Bloomingdale views
the Cheshire Cat as central to the work: "The central riddle of
Wonderland that must be solved is that which Alice asks the
Duchess concerning the Cheshire Cat: 'Please would you tell
me ... why your cat grins like that?' As the cat is traditionally
feminine (as the dog is masculine), the Cheshire Cat's presence
in the central, far-from-silent tableau of Wonderland, the emo-
tionally (pepper) charged kitchen of the Duchess's house, is
that of the Eternal Feminine. The mad grin of the appearing
and disappearing gargoyle, which literally 'hangs over' the heads
of the participants in the game of life, is an insane version of

the enigmatic smile of the 'Mona Lisa,' the mask of the Sphinx—
supreme embodiment of the riddle of the universe."[18] Bloomingdale may be correct in her interpretation of the symbolism of the
Cheshire Cat, but ironically, her articulation of its potency must
necessarily fall short of its subtle and mysterious effect upon
the reader.

When the Cat suddenly vanishes Alice is not much surprised.
Then it reappears to ask what became of the baby. Alice replies
that it turned into a pig and the Cat remarks, "I thought it
would" (p. 90) and vanishes. It is curious, indeed, that the Cat
would be concerned with the fate of the baby; and its lack of surprise that the boy turned into a pig suggests a disquieting omnis-
cience. The Cat vanishes and again reappears to ask if Alice said
"pig" or "fig," thereby undermining the presumed wisdom of its
earlier remark. As the chapter closes the Cat gradually vanishes
again—only this time its grin remains suspended among the
branches of its tree: " 'Well, I've often seen a cat without a grin,'
thought Alice; 'but a grin without a cat! It's the most curious
thing I ever saw in all my life' " (p. 91). As one critic has pointed
out "the seemingly indestructible bond between subject and
attribute—has been graphically subverted by the appearance of
a cat's grin without a cat."[19] Perhaps even more remarkable,
however, is Alice's coolness in the face of such a bizarre experience. The word "curious," the most frequent adjective used to
describe Alice's behavior, suggests a quiet, detached interest in
the occurrences surrounding her, an intellectual rather than an
emotional response to fantastic sights. It so happens that "curious"
is also the favorite word of Mr. Spock, an emotionless, almost
purely intellectual character on the popular television series
Star Trek. Like Mr. Spock, Alice is never amazed, excited, or
dreadfully afraid. In her own detached and amused aspect,
Alice is very much like the Cheshire Cat itself.

The Victorian tea party has its mad counterpart in Wonderland. Its madness is embodied in the character of the Hatter
who challenges Alice's sense of time, propriety, and logic. His
strategy is incomprehensible because it defies analysis, and his
remarks are as gratuitous as they are outrageous. After insulting
Alice for wearing her hair too long he abruptly poses a riddle.
In the disorder of Wonderland, which the Hatter's actions

encapsulate, transitions do not matter. Alice, the butt of Carroll's fun, has constantly to adapt to those around her, in this case from responding to personal insult to thinking of an answer to an answerless riddle, "Why is a raven like a writing-desk?" When Alice gives up and asks the Hatter the answer, he replies that he hasn't the slightest idea. Elizabeth Sewell suggests that the riddle should have no solution,[20] for it keeps the dream and disorder side of the mind in play. Carroll himself admitted that the riddle, as originally invented, had no answer at all. Once one comes up with an answer the nonsense, of course, disappears.

Having insulted Alice and presented her with an unanswerable riddle, the Hatter attacks her use of language. At one point the March Hare tells Alice to say what she means. She replies that "at least I mean what I say—that's the same thing, you know." But the Hatter retaliates with, "Not the same thing a bit! Why you might just as well say that 'I see what I eat' is the same thing as 'I eat what I see'!" (p. 95). As Roger W. Holmes points out, Carroll the philosopher-logician is at work here. "We know that if all apples are red, it does not follow that red things are apples: the logician's technical description of this is the non-convertability *simpliciter* of universal propositions."[21] Alice's sense of time as well as her grammar is undermined in the subsequent dialogue, which is full of puns based upon the nonsensical personification of time. Time itself is defined by and is an extension of the mad characteristics of the tea party. The scene Alice has come upon has no beginning and apparently no end. The personified time will not obey the Hatter; consequently it is always six o'clock, always tea time. The disordered conversation, like the ceaseless movement around the table, is endless.

In the midst of all this chaos is the sleepy dormouse whose imperturbability appears to anger the March Hare and the Hatter. When the Dormouse drowses off to sleep in the midst of its own story the Hatter pinches it, and as Alice walks off from the interminable madness she looks back and sees the Hare and Hatter trying to force the Dormouse into the teapot. There is no explanation offered for any of their actions, and since havoc is the rule here this piece of gratuitous violence is as good as any to conclude the chapter. Rackin believes that at this point in the narrative "the destruction of the foundations of Alice's old order is practically complete."[22] While it is true that most of the conventions which Alice—and the reader—subscribe to have been challenged and subverted by the inhabitants of Wonderland, it is not Alice but the reader who discovers this fact. In order to maintain the playful tension between the chaos of Wonderland and the conventionality of Alice, Carroll has to take care that Alice's understanding of her dream world does not develop, for that would bring an abrupt end to the nonsense. In this respect the nonsense is a form of irony implicit throughout the entire narrative.

The large rose tree that Alice finds in the Queen's croquet ground is an appropriate emblem of Wonderland; for it is painted red, thereby upsetting the traditional romantic image of the garden. At every turn in Wonderland the essential emotions of man are denied. Maternal love is translated into cruelty, compassion into rudeness, friendship into aloofness, and romance into sterile comedy. The gardeners, the courtiers, and the royalty that inhabit the garden are merely a pack of cards. Alice's final assertion of this fact frees her from Wonderland, but meanwhile she suffers their outrageous behavior.

The rose garden is a parodic garden of life. The only living creatures besides Alice are the flamingo, the hedgehog, and the Cheshire Cat, all animals. The "people" are cards. Furthermore, the flamingo and hedgehogs, which are living, are employed as surrogates for inanimate things, namely a croquet mallet and croquet balls. Life, as such, is inherently detrimental to the game of croquet where consistency and rigidity are required. Such consistency and rigidity, on the other hand, are to be found in the Queen of Hearts, who constantly calls out "Off with her head," and the King of Hearts, whose paper heart has long been trampled flat by his single-minded wife. As Alice says, "you've no idea how confusing it is all the things being alive" (p. 113). Against the threat of life to the game of croquet is the constant threat of death to Alice, the soldiers, and the Cheshire Cat. The Queen's cry for beheadings finally materializes in the person of the executioner who has been summoned to cut off the head of the Cat. Wonderland neutralizes its own tension at this point, for the Cheshire Cat's body has vanished, leaving only its grinning head and the metaphysical question, whether one can cut off a head when there is no body to cut it off from. Although the chapter ends with an academic consideration of execution, the subject of death has been strongly reinforced; but, like the other strong emotions, even the fear of death is turned into something else, in this case into a senseless intellectual argument.

At the outset of the next chapter Alice again meets the Duchess, who proves to be one of the most sinister characters in ·the book. The Duchess's preoccupation in finding morals in everything parodies the temper of the self-righteous moralists of Victorian England and ironically contrasts with her own sexual aggressiveness. Alice is made very uneasy by the Duchess's overtures: "Alice did not much like her keeping so close to her: first, because the Duchess was very ugly: and secondly, because she was exactly the right height to rest her chin on Alice's shoulder, and it was an uncomfortably sharp chin" (p. 120). When Alice remarks that the croquet game is going on rather better now, the Duchess who has "tucked her arm affectionately into Alice's" (p. 119) shifts the subject to romance: "'Tis so, and the moral of that is—'Oh, 'tis love, 'tis love, that makes the world go round!'" (p. 120). The Duchess proceeds to dig her sharp little chin further into Alice's shoulder and says, "I dare say you're wondering why I don't put my arm round your waist" (p. 121). Since Alice is still carrying her flamingo, the Duchess suggests that "I'm doubtful about the temper of your flamingo. Shall I try the experiment?" "He might bite" (p. 121), Alice cautiously replies, not at all interested in the experiment. In the midst of subsequent banter the Duchess continues to dig her chin into Alice's shoulder until the Queen arrives and threatens to chop off her head unless she be off.

William Empson interprets this episode as follows: "The scene ... shows Alice no longer separate from her creator; it is clear that Dodgson would be as irritated as she is by the incident, and is putting himself in her place. The obvious way to read it is as the middle-aged woman trying to flirt with the chaste young man."[23] How obvious that reading is is questionable, but Empson has a point about Carroll's uneasy treatment of sex in this scene. The Duchess's quiet and escalating sexual overtures seem sinister, and the episode becomes more disturbing than even Empson suggests when one simply takes it as a subtle attempt of a grotesque old woman to seduce an innocent child. Some of the dialogue, of course, reflects the submerged sexuality. Alice's flamingo "might bite" if the Duchess tries her "experiment." The word "experiment" to describe putting her arm around Alice's waist is possibly a sinister euphemism for her seduction.

The satire on didacticism noted in Alice's second encounter with the Duchess is explored fully by Leach: "In this episode, the Duchess's motto is 'Everything's got a moral, if only you can find it,' and she becomes more and more extravagant and nonsensical in her application of axioms to everything Alice says and does. When Dodgson makes a ridiculous character like the Duchess praise and practice moralizing in this manner, he clearly indicates his attitude toward didacticism directed against children."[24] Leach goes on to speculate whether Carroll consciously had in mind the popular children's book by Oliver Goldsmith, *Little Goody Two Shoes.* In that work the wise and mature heroine Margery "had the art of moralizing and drawing instructions from every accident, as when the death of a pet dormouse gave her the opportunity of reading them (the children) a lecture on the uncertainty of life, and the necessity of being always prepared for death."[25]

Free from the Duchess Alice next meets the Mock Turtle and the Gryphon, two sentimentalists, who, according to Gardner, are "obvious satires on the sentimental college alumnus, of which Oxford has always had an unusually large share."[26] Whereas most of the Wonderland creatures are lacking in the emotions of love, compassion, or friendship, these two characters in their excessive show of feeling are as sterile and shallow as their mad fellows. At last, it seems, Alice has found someone with whom she can actually communicate. They ask her about her previous adventures; and she describes them up to her meeting with the Caterpillar, at which point the Gryphon says, "It's all about as curious as it can be" (p. 138). Then the Turtle asks her to repeat "'Tis the voice of the sluggard" to see if it will come out different, as "Father William" had in the presence of the Caterpillar. These are hardly reassuring responses to

Alice's story, for they merely involve her in still another bizarre adventure. The suggestion in Alice's recitation that the panther feasted on the owl is apparently lost on the Mock Turtle, who complains, "What *is* the use of repeating all that stuff if you don't explain it as you go on?" (p. 140). Humpty Dumpty, in *Through the Looking-Glass*, stands at the opposite extreme in his ability to explicate all poems, even those not written yet. The theme of eating, in any case, is continued in the Mock Turtle's song about beautiful soup. His voice is naturally choked with sobs, for his potential essence is soup. The leisurely mawkish song is interrupted by the cry, "The trial's beginning." The sense of urgency introduced here carries the reader back to the beginning of Alice's adventures when she overheard the White Rabbit saying "Oh dear! Oh dear! I shall be too late!"

The time-obsessed White Rabbit appears again in Chapter XI, with a trumpet in one hand and a scroll in the other, standing near the King. Many of the creatures assembled at the court Alice has met before, suggesting a final assemblage for the approaching conclusion. The conduct of the judge, jurors, and witnesses is, not surprisingly, totally uncivilized. Insignificant details are stressed and important ones overlooked. Justice is as arbitrary as it is whimsical. Rackin says that what is on trial is the law itself.[27] There is no law in Wonderland, nothing can be systematically evaluated. Wonderland indiscriminately introduces chaos into everything it touches, from the game of croquet to legal trials. And as in the Queen's croquet grounds, the threat of execution is constantly present in the courtroom.

The trial is seen as an allegorical comment on the Oxford Movement by Shane Leslie. He argues as follows: the tarts represent the Thirty-Nine Articles of the Anglican faith; a "knavish Ritualist" (John Henry Newman) is accused of "having removed their natural sense"; and the Mad Hatter (High Church) and the March Hare (Low Church) are called as witnesses against him. Leslie concludes: "it is interesting that the King's words to the Knave were exactly those which had been hurled at Newman and at everybody who had tried to equivocate on the Articles. 'You must have meant some mischief or else you would have signed your name like an honest man.' "[28] It is not impossible, of course, that Carroll was thinking of Newman in this section, but the artistic success of *Wonderland* obviously does not derive from its allegorical-satirical nature, since the modern reader is no longer concerned with the Oxford Movement.

The reigning chaos of the trial begins to be endangered by Alice's growing size. She upsets the jury box, spilling the animals onto the floor. The King objects that the trial cannot proceed until all the jurymen are back in their proper places. Such pointless formality in the midst of gross disorder is commonplace at this point; but Alice is beginning to rebel, and her increasing size threatens Wonderland with the ultimate disorder—annihilation. The Queen calls for the Knave of Hearts to be sentenced before the jury submits their verdict. Alice challenges the Queen with "Stuff and nonsense!", a statement that dangerously threatens to unravel the substance of Wonderland. When the Queen shouts "Off with her head!" Alice makes her climactic protest: "Who cares for *you*? You're nothing but a pack of cards!" (p. 161). With this exclamation she annihilates Wonderland as if by word magic, and the suspension of disbelief is at an end. In Alice's calling the bluff of the Queen, one critic sees "the underlying message of Alice," namely, the "rejection of adult authority, a vindication of the rights of the child, even the right of the child to self-assertion."[29]

Contrasting with the uncertainties and anxieties of Wonderland is Alice's sister's idyllic imagination: "Lastly she pictured to herself how this same little sister of hers would, in the aftertime, be herself a grown woman; and how she would keep, through all her riper years, the simple and loving heart of her childhood" (p. 164). The nightmarish tone of the story changes at the conclusion into sentimentality and an idyllic affirmation of innocence. This peaceful conclusion, with its hope for the preservation of Alice's simple joys and childhood innocence, grows directly out of the rest of the work. Implicit throughout the adventures is Alice's inviolable innocence, an innocence shaped and graced by the standards of Victorian morality. She has met and withstoood all the challenges of Wonderland and emerges from her dream world totally unaware of the significance of her journey. Equipped with conventional expectations, proper manners, and a moral superiority, Alice possesses a purity that is unassailable in Wonderland and promises, as her sister's dream suggests, to remain that way in the real world. She could thus cope with the rudeness of the Hatter, the sexual overtures of the Duchess; but her own body, and its changing size, presented a real difficulty. The codes of ethics and good manners failed to explain how she should handle this problem—and consequently she is led into still another puzzle, namely, who or what is she? The book is obviously concerned with the subject of growing up, but the focus is upon the anxieties of maturity and the mystery of one's true identity. The anxieties are there in the work, stressed particularly in the Caterpillar's rough questioning of Alice, but Carroll the narrator does not deal with the subject in a controlled way. It is almost as if, once recognizing the pain of growth, he refuses to follow out its implications—for that would be to make Alice's character develop, to replace her innocence with the sexuality of adolescence. The dream of Alice's sister, then, is the dream of Carroll himself, who in his anticipation of Alice Liddell's maturity may well echo the conclusion of the book, that Alice would "find a pleasure in all their [other children's] simple joys, remembering her own child-life, and the happy summer days" (p. 164).

II   Through the Looking-Glass

Jan B. Gordon has observed that *Alice's Adventures in Wonderland* stands to *Through the Looking-Glass* as play stands to artifice.[30] He notes that the latter story takes place indoors in autumn, whereas its predecessor takes place outdoors in spring. Alice says to her Kitten in the former work, "Let's pretend the glass has got all soft like gauze, so that we can get through" (pp. 181–82); such contrived artifice does not appear in *Wonderland*. In the first book the emphasis is upon Alice's adventures and what happens to her on the experiential level; in the sequel the reader accepts Alice and with detachment examines nature transformed in the artifice of Looking-Glass Land. The voyage has shifted from the Kingdom of Chaos, with its riotous motion and verbal whirlpool, to the land of stasis, where the landscape is geometrical and the chessmen are carefully manipulated by the rules of a precise game. In Wonderland everybody says and does whatever comes into his head, but in the Looking-

Glass world life is completely determined and without choice. Tweedledum and Tweedledee, the Lion and the Unicorn, the Red Knight and the White must fight at regular intervals, whether they want to or not.

References to determinism suggest philosophical implications. After the White Knight has fallen off his horse for the ninth time and is dangling head downwards, Alice asks him how he can go on talking so quietly from that position. He replies, "What does it matter where my body happens to be? My mind goes on working all the time" (p. 304). As Roger Holmes points out, his response clearly reflects the Cartesian dualism of Mind and Body.[31] There is an allusion to the philosophy of Bishop Berkeley in the following dialogue about the Red King:

"He's dreaming now," said Tweedledee, "and what do you think he's dreaming about?"

Alice said, "Nobody can guess that."

"Why, about you!" Tweedledee explained, clapping his hands triumphantly. "And if he left off dreaming about you, where do you suppose you'd be?"

"Where I am now, of course," said Alice.

"Not you!" Tweedledee retorted contemptuously. "You'd be no-where. Why, you're only a sort of thing in his dream!"

"If that there King was to wake," added Tweedledum, "you'd go out—bang!—just like a candle!" (p. 238)

Holmes notes that the Red King performs the function of God in the philosophy of Berkeley. To be is to be perceived, ultimately in the mind of God—or the Red King. When Alice tells the twins to keep quiet lest they wake the King, Tweedledum answers, "Well, it's no use *your* talking about waking him when you're only one of the things in his dream. You know very well you're not real" (p. 239). Tweedledum raises the central problem of philosophy, the problem of the nature of reality and the threat of the subjectivity of knowledge.[32]

There are numerous other allusions to philosophy throughout the book, but the point to observe here is that such references make the texture of Looking-Glass world much more abstract, problematic, and deterministic than that of Wonderland. Whether it be the Red King or the unseen chess master there is a sense of controlled order and determination here. Although there are a few vague intimations of such manipulation in Wonderland, such as the mysterious appearance of the "Drink Me" bottle upon the table (Alice noted that it "certainly was not here before"), the essential spontaneity of Alice's adventures and encounters in Wonderland is never seriously impaired by exterior forces. She is totally free to go where she pleases and do what she desires. Having lived with disorder, she now must come to grips with strict rules and unyielding order.

Patricia Spacks says that Carroll's world of fantasy, in its semantic aspects at least, is "the sort of world for which such a logician as Charles Dodgson might yearn: a world of truth and order."[33] That it seems disorderly, she argues, is a condemnation of the ordinary sloppy thinking of the reader and the sloppy traditions of his language. There are several forces of control and order in Looking-Glass Land besides the chess rules, and one of the most important is language itself. Language relates things in this well-ordered world. For example, Alice is told that when danger comes to the tree in the garden the tree barks—it says "bough-wough." In the actual world there is obviously no relationship between the bark of a tree, the bark of a dog or between "bow-wow" and "bough-wough." Our use of language is more arbitrary and unaccountable than that of Looking-Glass Land. The Frog, for example, cannot understand why anyone should answer the door unless it has been asking something. Francis Bacon, like the Frog, also mistrusted words that were "confused and ill-defined, and hastily and irregularly derived from realities"; and his essays led the Royal Society to cultivate a plain, stripped prose style for purposes of scientific communication. Bacon would have approved the semantic logic of Looking-Glass Land.

Sometimes language has the power of primitive magic to make things happen. Alice is able to walk with her arm around the neck of a fawn through the mysterious woods where names are forgotten. When names return to the two on the far side of the wood, the fawn runs away in fear. (An interesting modern parallel to this is found in Bernardo Bertolucci's *Last Tango in Paris*, where Paul and Jeanne maintain a sexual relationship in an apartment where names are banned. When the apartment is abandoned and they take on names and personalities their relationship begins to deteriorate and ends in Jeanne's shooting Paul.) The power of the word is also seen in the nursery rhyme. Tweedledee and Tweedledum fight over the rattle not because they want to but because the rhyme says they do, and so they must. Language determines actions with all the force of a deity. Humpty Dumpty knows that if he falls the king will send all his horses and men to pick him up because the rhyme says so. The Lion and the Unicorn will fight for the crown and the action will continue to the drumming out of town—again, because the rhyme says so.

Another force of determinism in Looking-Glass Land is the chessboard itself. The game is not strictly up to chess standards because Carroll was more interested in the implications of the game and its moves than he was in working out the actual game. Alexander Taylor points out that since Alice is a pawn she can only see a small patch of board and, consequently, can not understand the meaning of her experiences: "This is a pawn's impression of chess, which is like a human being's impressions of life." "Alice never grasps the purpose of the game at all," Taylor continues, "and when she reaches the Eighth Square tries to find out from the two Queens if it is over. None of the pieces has the least idea what it is all about."[34] An understanding of one's role in a game of chess would entail an awareness of the room and the unseen intelligence that is manipulating the counters. At no time does Alice converse with a piece that is not then on a square alongside her own. Even the eccentric behavior of the engaging White Knight reflects the eccentric way in which Knights move. The fact that he keeps falling from his horse suggests the Knight's move of two squares in one direction followed by one square to the right or left. The chess game also reinforces the mirror-reflection motif. Not only do many of the pieces come in pairs but the asymmetric arrangement of one player's pieces at the start of the game is an exact mirror reflection of his opponent's pieces.[35] If, then, as Elizabeth Sewell has said, the chief aim of the game of Nonsense is to create a universe which will be logical and orderly, *Through the Looking-Glass* is more purely nonsense than *Alice's Adventures in Wonderland*.

The principle of inversion (do cats eat bats or do bats eat cats), which supplied some of the humor of *Alice's Adventures*, is a dominant force in Looking-Glass world: Alice must walk backwards in order to approach the Red Queen; the White Queen explains the advantages of living backward in time; and the White Knight thinks best when seeing things upside down. Carroll also enjoyed inverting things in real life. He would compose letters in mirror-writing that had to be held to a mirror to be read. He wrote letters that had to be read by starting from the last word and reading to the first. Related to this technique is the humor of logical contradictions: Alice runs as fast as she can to stay in the same place; the Red Queen offers Alice a biscuit to quench her thirst; and the Unicorn is amazed that Alice is alive and not a fabulous monster. The paradoxical progress in Alice's running can be explained as a mathematical trick: "In our world speed is the ratio of distance to time: $s = d \div t$. For a high speed, the distance is great and the time is small; so many miles per hour. Through the Looking-glass, however, speed is the ratio of time to distance: $s = t \div d$. For a high speed, the time is great and the distance small. The higher the speed, the smaller the distance covered."[36] Another aspect of such logic twisting is Carroll's treatment of nothing as something: Alice wonders where the flame of a candle is when the candle is not burning; the White Knight praises Alice's keen vision in being able to see nobody down the road; and the King of Hearts finds it unusual to write letters to nobody.[37]

Reminiscent of her experiences in Wonderland, Alice is treated rather shabbily and rudely by the inhabitants of Looking-Glass Land. Alice may be in the tradition of the great Victorian explorers who make adventure an end in itself, but she is also an intruder and can never be at home in the two alien worlds she visits. As explorer, Alice bears the stamp of the English imperialist: her civilized social assumptions allow her to elevate the tone of the foreign world she enters, a task that is simplified by the rudeness of the creatures she meets. Empson observes that Alice is both aristocratic and snobbish and as "the perfect lady" she "can gain all the advantages of contempt without soiling herself by expressing or even feeling it."[38] The rude reception she receives in the Garden of Live Flowers makes it clear from the outset that she is going to be in for hard times. The Victorians, who did so much to sentimentalize flowers in poetry, song and paintings, now have vengeance wreaked upon them in the person of Alice.

Alice continually approaches a sense of unity with nature in her adventures: she can converse with flowers, insects, animals, and inanimate objects such as cards and chessmen. Yet, unlike Wordsworth's child of glory, Alice always remains detached, isolated, and self-protective.[39] Despite the humor in her dialogue with the Gnat, there is the subtle undercurrent of the reality of death. She asks what the Bread-and-butter-fly lives on, to which the Gnat replies, "Weak tea with cream in it." "Supposing it couldn't find any?" asks Alice. "Then it would die, of course," answers the Gnat—"it always happens" (p. 223). At the end of their conversation, the Gnat sighs itself away, vanishing completely like the Baker in the *Snark*, and the only response that Alice can make is to get up and walk on. Implanted in her mind now is the philosophically complex question of the relationship of one's name to one's being. She becomes in the wood in which things have no names a pure child of nature, walking with her arms clasped lovingly around the neck of a fawn. But this pastoral bliss is quickly dispelled as they emerge from the wood and the fawn recognizes Alice to be a human child: "a sudden look of alarm came into its beautiful brown eyes, and in another moment it had darted away at full speed" (p. 227). Alice watches it run away and is "almost ready to cry with vexation at having lost her dear little fellow-traveller so suddenly" (p. 227). Once again, the tentative unity with nature is breached and Alice is left with only one comfort—she regains her name.

Tweedledum and Tweedledee extend the artifice of Looking-Glass Land in that they are mirror-image forms of each other. Tweedledee's favorite word, "contrariwise," and the fact that the brothers extend right and left hands for a handshake reinforce the mirror-image motif. In putting forth the Berkeleyian view that all material objects, including Alice, are only "sorts of things" in the mind of the Red King (God) they further the theme of determinism. Not only does man relinquish free will but his essence is indistinct from his creator's: he is a mere fiction shaped by a dreaming mind. Moments earlier Alice lost her name, and now the reality of her actual being is brought into question. Confounded at first, Alice begins to cry but then asserts that if she were not real she could not cry. Tweedledum contemptuously replies that her tears are false, and Alice finally resolves that the brothers are talking nonsense. The ultimate question of what is real and what is dream, however, is never resolved in the book. In fact, the story ends with the perplexing question of who dreamed it all—Alice or the Red King? Presumably, Alice dreamed of the King, who is dreaming of Alice, who is dreaming of the King, and so on. As Gardner points out, the question of dream versus reality is set forth in terms of an infinite regression through mirror facing mirror.[40]

In keeping with the looking-glass principles of logical inversion and contradiction, the White Queen introduces Alice to some of the details of living backwards: here one remembers things that happened the week after next; the King's Messenger is imprisoned, then his trial takes place, and finally he commits the crime. Such a weird chronology strengthens the determinism of looking-glass world. The Queen's finger, for example, begins bleeding, and she then recollects that she will soon prick it on the brooch that fastens her shawl. For every effect, there must obviously come about a cause.

Even as the Duchess's child had turned into a pig, so now the White Queen becomes a sheep and, as if by dream magic, Alice finds herself in a shop. Shortly thereafter the sheep's knitting needles turn into oars, and Alice finds herself rowing a boat with the old sheep through the queer shop. After some punning on rowing slang, the boating couple land on some rushes, the sheep moves to the other end of the shop (in chess terms, the White Queen moves to KB8), and Alice comes into the presence of Humpty Dumpty. Empson suggests that the sheep represents Oxford and the life of learning: "Everyone recognizes the local shop, the sham fights, the rowing, the academic old Sheep, and the way it laughs scornfully when Alice doesn't know the technical slang of rowing."[41] The dream-like fading of Queen into sheep, knitting needles into oars, and the sudden appearance of the boat not only counterpoint the rigid geometry of Looking-Glass world, but remind the reader that the entire adventure is encapsulated in a dream.

The episode with Humpty Dumpty is a comic essay on language and comments more extensively on the earlier episode of the wood with no names. Applying the principle of inversion, Humpty makes clear that ordinary words mean whatever he wants them to mean ("glory" for example, means "a nice knock-down argument"), whereas proper names are supposed to have general significance (Humpty explains that his name means the shape he is). In actuality, of course, the reverse is usually true. Humpty assumes the nominalist position that universal terms do not have an objective existence but are mere verbal utterances: "When *I* use a word it means just what I choose it to mean—neither more nor less" (p. 269). When Alice questions whether he can make words mean so many different things, he replies "the question is, which is to be master—that's all" (p. 269). In *Symbolic Logic* Carroll argued that every author may establish his own definitions: "... any writer of a book is fully authorised in attaching any meaning he likes to any word or phrase he intends to use. If I find an author saying, at the beginning of his book, 'Let it be understood that by the word *black* I shall always mean *white*, and that by the word *white* I shall always mean *black*,' I meekly accept this ruling, however injudicious I may think it."[42]

Beyond these serious philosophical and linguistic issues raised by Humpty's dissertation on words, an essential point not to be overlooked is that he is authoritarian, pedantic, and a fourth-rate literary critic. As J. B. Priestly has pointed out, "he thinks that every simple question is a riddle, something for him to solve triumphantly."[43] In Humpty Dumpty's discussion of Alice's age he shows himself to be annoyingly pedantic and his expli-cation of "Jabberwocky" displays a foolish self-assurance: "I can explain all the poems that ever were invented—and a good many that haven't been invented just yet" (p. 270).

Even in the midst of Humpty's pedantic discourse on words the idea of death is not far off. His remark to Alice is, indeed, shocking:

"Seven years and six months!" Humpty Dumpty repeated thought-fully. "'An uncomfortable sort of age. Now if you'd asked my advice, I'd have said, 'Leave off at seven'—but it's too late now."

"I never ask advice about growing," Alice said indignantly. "Too proud?" the other inquired.

Alice felt even more indignant at this suggestion. "I mean," she said, "That one can't help growing older."

"*One* can't, perhaps," said Humpty Dumpty; "but *two* can. With proper assistance you might have left off at seven."

"What a beautiful belt you've got on!" Alice suddenly remarked.

(pp. 265–66)

Humpty's chilling phrase, "with proper assistance," is a grim reminder that Alice dwells in a post lapserian world and that her innocence is indeed a fragile commodity. Implied in Humpty's remark is A. E. Housman's compliment, "Smart lad, to slip betimes away / From fields where glory does not stay."

With the appearance of the White Knight Alice discovers for the first time someone who seems to be genuinely fond of her and who treats her with courtesy and respect. Many critics have suggested that Carroll intended the White Knight to be a caricature of himself. Gardner draws some of the similarities: "Like the knight, Carroll had shaggy hair, mild blue eyes, a kind and gentle face. Like the knight, his mind seemed to function best when it saw things in topsy-turvy fashion. Like the knight, he was fond of curious gadgets and was a 'great hand at inventing things.' "[44] Another critic sees the White Knight in mythic terms: "This is the mystical moment for Alice. Not her own coronation, but that of the true King of the Looking-Glass World. Not a mighty world conqueror, but the gentle man, the pure and innocent hero, the risen Christ radiant with scars— Christ as Clown."[45] Still another critic sees him as a parody of the Victorian scientist who "earnestly, patiently, carefully . . . without sensuality, without self-seeking, without claiming any but a fragment of knowledge . . . goes on laboring at his absurd but fruitful conceptions."[46]

The knight is equipped with gadgets to handle almost any imaginable contingency: a mouse-trap to keep mice from running about his horse, anklets around the horse's feet to ward off shark bites, an upside down little box for his clothes and sandwiches. His sad farewell to Alice suggests Carroll's own farewell to Alice Liddell when she grew up and left him. Alice's progress towards becoming a queen is indicative of such growth:

"You've only a few yards to go," he said, "—down the hill and over that little brook, and then you'll be a Queen—But you'll stay and see me off first?" he added as Alice turned with an eager look in the direction to which he pointed, "I shan't be long. You'll wait and wave your handkerchief when I get to that turn in the road! I think it'll encourage me, you see!" (pp. 313–14)

Alice's youthful eagerness to be crowned Queen quickly extinguishes from her mind the affectionate image of the White Knight. After waving her handkerchief to him, she says: " 'I hope it encouraged him,' as she turned to run down the hill: 'and now for the last brook, and to be a Queen! How grand it sounds!' " (p. 314). Such youthful ambition for pastures new is a true valediction forbidding weeping.

Alice finally leaps the one remaining brook (square) and changes from a pawn to a queen. Although still controlled by the rules of the chessboard, as queen she assumes a great new power through freedom of movement. The Red and White Queens, however, set out to give Alice an examination that will rightfully allow her to assume the new title. After badgering her with outrageous questions the two queens fall asleep. Alice then goes through an archway marked "Queen Alice," enters a large banquet hall filled with animals, birds, flowers, and the two revived queens. The chapter moves towards a finale that strongly suggests that Alice's coronation is tantamount to a sexual orgasm (she "mates" the King): "The candles all grew up to the ceiling, looking something like a bed of rushes with fireworks at the top. As to the bottles, they each took a pair of plates, which they hastily fitted on as wings, and so, with forks for legs, went fluttering about in all directions" (p. 335). As she afterwards recalled, "all sorts of things happened in a moment" (p. 335) ("moment" being a much repeated word in the last few paragraphs). The intensity of this moment finally overwhelms Alice and she ends the dream (hers or the Red King's): "I can't stand this any longer" (p. 336), she shouts, and seizes the tablecloth and pulls the plates, guests, and candles down into a crashing heap upon the floor. In chess terms, Alice has captured the Red Queen and checkmates the sleeping Red King. In human terms, she has grown up and entered that fated condition of puberty, at which point Carroll dismisses her once and for all by concluding his story.

III   *Through Bergson's Looking Glass*

Scholars, critics, psychoanalysts, and logicians have all scrutinized Carroll's writings; but few of them have offered an explanation of why or how his creations are funny. The problem with any serious discussion of humor, of course, is that the analysis inevitably destroys the fun. How much easier it is to elucidate Hamlet's melancholy than to explain Falstaff's jokes! Nevertheless, humor is at the very heart of Carroll's major works, and no discussion of them could be complete without an examination of some of the principles of that humor, especially as they apply to Alice.

Henri Bergson's essay on *Laughter,* published in 1900, is a classic statement of the principles of humor, and is especially relevant to the comedy of manners. His observations, however, are very pertinent to Carroll's humor as well. Like Carroll, Bergson lived through the technological revolution that made the duality of man and machine a vital concern of philosophers, novelists, poets, and humorists. One living in the middle and late 1800's could retreat from, attack, make a compromise with, or poke fun at the frightening rise of technology. Bergson believed that life is a vital impulse, not to be understood by reason alone, and sees the comical as something encrusted on the living.

Early in his essay Bergson makes the interesting observation that laughter and emotion are incompatible: "It seems as though the comic could not produce its disturbing effect unless it fell, so to say, on the surface of a soul that is thoroughly calm and unruffled. Indifference is its natural environment, for laughter has no greater foe than emotion."[47] In both his comic poetry and prose Carroll maintains a fairly consistent detachment from his characters, and his characters likewise usually remain remarkably detached from their environment. Alice, for example, forms no strong or lasting relationships with any of the creatures or persons of Wonderland and Looking-Glass Land, with the notable exception of the White Knight. And the scene in which Alice bids farewell to the White Knight is clearly not funny because there is an emotional bond between them. The Cheshire Cat is the

obvious symbol of intellectual detachment, its grin suggestive
of an amused observer. It can appear as only a head for it is
representative of a disembodied intelligence.

A sentimentalist might have difficulty in appreciating comedy
for, as Bergson notes, "to produce the whole of its effect ... the
comic demands something like a momentary anesthesia of the
heart. Its appeal is to intelligence, pure and simple" (p. 63).
Carroll's parodies of the didactic and sentimental verses of Isaac
Watts, for example, are funny in so far as the reader is aware
of the originals and attentive to the intellectual cleverness
involved in reshaping them. The emotions that the moral senti-
ments originally invoked are repressed by the wit of the parodies.
What might pass for cruelty in the treatment Alice receives in
Wonderland is, in fact, funny because the emotions are excluded.
Alice's conversation with Humpty Dumpty is a case in point:
" 'I mean,' she said, 'that one ca'n't help growing older.' "One
ca'n't, perhaps," said Humpty Dumpty; 'but *two* can. With
proper assistance, you might have left off at seven.' " Despite the
fact that Humpty Dumpty is suggesting that Alice might have
been killed off at age seven (not a very funny idea), the passage is humorous because Carroll's focus is clearly upon Humpty
Dumpty's linguistic playfulness—his intelligence and wit—and
not upon Alice's death. One could apply Bergson's observation
to countless examples in Carroll's works, from "The Two
Brothers" to *The Hunting of the Snark*, and his principle holds
up. We are not sickened at witnessing a boy using his brother
as bait ("The Two Brothers") any more than we grieve over
the annihilation of the Baker (*The Hunting of the Snark*). Carroll
rarely allows us to know well and sympathize with his characters
and thereby spares us an emotional reaction when they are
assailed.

Bergson refines his observation that laughter appeals to intelligence pure and simple by adding, "this intelligence, however,
must always remain in touch with other intelligences." He continues: "The comic will come into being, it appears, whenever
a group of men concentrate their attention on one of their
number, imposing silence on their emotions and calling into
play nothing but their intelligence" (p. 65). Alice provides
exactly that focus of concentration for the reader. She is the

instrument of humor as Carroll the narrator engages the mind of the reader to share with him the absurdity that arises in her various encounters with the creatures of Wonderland. Carroll invites the reader to conspire with him to laugh at their mutual representative battling with foreign intelligences.

Basic to Bergson's conception of the comic is the tension that exists between rigidity and suppleness: "rigidity is the comic, and laughter is its corrective" (p. 74). He sees a laughable expression of the face as "one that promises nothing more than it gives. It is a unique and permanent grimace. One would say that the person's whole moral life has crystallised into this particular cast of features" (p. 76). He concludes that "automatism, *inelasticity*, habit that has been contracted and maintained are clearly the causes why a face makes us laugh" (p. 76). Tenniel's illustrations are significant in this respect, for they help to fix the expressions of such characters as the Cheshire Cat with its sinister grin and the Queen of Hearts with her perpetual scowl. The Queen's favorite expression, "Off with his head!" or "Off with her head!" likewise is as fixed and predictable as her expression. The sentiment is obviously not funny, but its repetition is.

In more general terms both Alice books deal with the battle between rigidity and suppleness. Alice embodies secure conventions and self-assured regulations, and Wonderland is dedicated to undermining those conventions and regulations. Herein lies the validity of Derek Hudson's observation that Carroll's comic method is similar to that of the Marx Brothers, a reckless team dead set on overthrowing conventions of civilized behavior. In Looking-Glass Land the rigid rules of chess are set against the relatively undisciplined behavior of humans, thereby reversing the situation in Wonderland. In this connection another statement by Bergson is revealing: *"The attitudes, gestures and movements of the human body are laughable in exact proportion as that body reminds us of a mere machine"* (p. 79). In *Through the Looking-Glass* Alice and the other characters are treated as chess pieces to be manipulated in a very rational game. In short, they have become things and, as Bergson notes, *"we laugh every time a person gives us the impression of being a thing"* (p. 97). Similarly, the repetitive battles between Tweedledee and Tweedledum are comic because they are predictable.

Discussing the humor of disguise, Bergson argues that "any image . . . suggestive of the notion of a society disguising itself, or of a social masquerade, so to speak, will be laughable" (p. 89). The humor lies in the conflict between the rigidity of ceremony and conventions with the "inner suppleness of life." A ceremony becomes comic, he continues, when our attention is fixed on the ceremonial element in it, and "we neglect its matter, as philosophers say, and think only of its form" (p. 89). Both the Caucus-race and the trial of the Knave of Hearts illustrate Bergson's thesis. In the former, all the contestants are awarded prizes, thereby ignoring the substance of the race, namely, finding a winner. In the trial scene, the procedures are of paramount importance, the guilt or innocence of the defendant being of little significance. In both cases a kind of relentless automatism rules supreme that converts human beings into comic puppets.

One final observation by Bergson has relevance to Carroll's humor: "*Any incident is comic that calls our attention to the physical in a person, when it is the moral side that is concerned*" (p. 93). The humor resides in one's perceiving the tension in a "soul tantalised by the needs of the body: on the one hand, the moral personality with its intelligently varied energy, and, on the other, the stupidly monotonous body, perpetually obstructing everything with its machine-like obstinacy" (p. 93). Thus, he argues, we laugh at a public speaker who sneezes just at the most pathetic moment of his speech. Our attention is suddenly recalled from the soul to the body. Alice's frustrations in regulating her body size are cases in point. She longs to enter into "the loveliest garden you ever saw" but "she could not even get her head through the doorway." There are numerous passages in the Alice books, not to mention Carroll's other works, in which the human body baffles, betrays and embarrasses the soul.

One of the functions of humor, as Bergson saw it, was to make us human and natural during an age of mechanization. In spite of, perhaps because of, his own compulsiveness and rigidity, Carroll truly fulfilled that function in his writings. One of Carroll's early poems, "Rules and Regulations," establishes that at the outset of his career he both prized and mocked rigidity.

He recognized that the machinery of conventions and customs, mathematics and logic, helped to define by contrast the mutable, comic, imperfect creature called man.

CHAPTER 5

Sylvie and Bruno
and
Sylvie and Bruno Concluded

IN 1867 Carroll wrote a short children's story entitled "Bruno's Revenge" for *Aunt Judy's Magazine*. This fairy tale served as the nucleus for the novel *Sylvie and Bruno*, which Carroll worked on intermittently for over fifteen years: "It was in 1874, I believe, that the idea first occurred to me of making it the nucleus of a longer story. As the years went on, I jotted down, at odd moments, all sorts of odd ideas, and fragments of dialogue, that occurred to me—who knows how?—With a transitory suddenness that left me no choice but either to record them then and there, or to abandon them to oblivion." He goes on to declare in the preface that it would be courting disaster to revert to the style of the Alice books: "Hence it is that, in 'Sylvie and Bruno,' I have striven—with I know not what success—to strike out yet another new path: be it bad or good, it is the best I can do."[1]

Carroll's interest in spiritualism was a crucial factor in his writing *Sylvie and Bruno*. He joined the Society for Psychical Research a year after its founding in 1882 and retained his membership until the year before his death. He owned numerous books about spiritualism and the occult, including Daniel Dunglas Home's *Lights and Shadows of Spiritualism*, Vernon Lee's *Other World*, Alfred Wallace's *Miracles and Modern Spiritualism*, O. R. H. Thomson's *Philosophy of Magic*, Christmas's *Phantom World*, Frank Seafield's *Literature and Curiosities of Dreams*, and Edward Clodd's *Myths and Dreams*. Carroll's interest in the spirit world goes back, of course, well past the 1880's; but in his earlier writings, such as *Phantasmagoria* (1869), he treated the subject more flippantly.

112

In the preface to *Sylvie and Bruno Concluded* (1893) he outlined the hypothesis upon which the story is based: "It is an attempt to show what might *possibly* happen, supposing that Fairies really existed; and that they were sometimes visible to us, and we to them; and that they were sometimes able to assume human form: and supposing, also, that human beings might sometimes become conscious of what goes on in the Fairy-world—by actual tranference of their immaterial essence, such as we meet with in Esoteric Buddhism."[2] As he grew older Carroll began to adopt a form of Christian Platonism. In one of his letters he states, "I find that as life slips away (I am over fifty now) and the life on the other side of the great river becomes more and more the reality, of which *this* is only a shadow, that the petty distinctions of the many creeds of Christianity tend to slip away as well—leaving only the great truths all Christians believe alike."[3] In *Sylvie and Bruno* Carroll presents these two worlds and unites them through the gospel of love, which he offers as the essential Christian truth.

Carroll lists three psychical states exhibited by the various characters in his story. First, there is "the ordinary state," which precludes an awareness of Fairies. Second is the "eerie state," in which, while one is conscious of actual surroundings, he is also conscious of the presence of Fairies. And third, there is "a form of trance," in which, while unconscious of actual surroundings and apparently asleep, one's immaterial essence migrates to other scenes, in the actual world or in Fairyland, and is conscious of the presence of Fairies.[4] The anonymous narrator of the two Bruno stories experiences all three states at one time or another.

I *Structure*

It is difficult to summarize the story of *Sylvie and Bruno* because the narrator keeps drifting from the actual world to the fairy world. One can see parallels between the inhabitants and events of both worlds and occasionally a conflation of the two. The plot that deals with the human characters is a simple one. A brilliant young doctor named Arthur Forster falls in love with Lady Muriel Orme, the daughter of an affectionate old Earl. Because of some financial difficulties and, more important, because he feels that Lady Muriel is beyond his reach, Arthur hesitates to declare his love for her. Meanwhile Lady Muriel's handsome young cousin, the Honorable Eric Lindon, arrives on the scene and they become engaged. His hopes crushed, Arthur prepares to leave England for India where he has been offered a medical appointment. The book ends with a poetical invocation: "From the East comes new strength, new ambition, new Hope, new Life, new Love! Look Eastward! Aye, look Eastward!"[5] In *Sylvie and Bruno Concluded* Carroll manages to bring Lady Muriel and Arthur together. Lady Muriel breaks off her engagement to Eric on theological grounds, their differences being hinted at in the last chapter of *Sylvie and Bruno*. With the help of the invisible sprites, Sylvie and Bruno, Arthur's love for Lady Muriel is fulfilled in marriage.

The second plot involves the invisible world. A realm named Outland is ruled by a Warden who withdraws from his governmental duties in order to go upon a journey disguised as a beggar. The Sub-Warden and his ugly wife conspire with the Chancellor to usurp the Warden's power. This plot is unresolved in the first novel, but in *Sylvie and Bruno Concluded* the Warden returns to punish the conspirators and to proclaim the Empire of Love, an empire which is reflected in the actual world by the love between Lady Muriel and Arthur.

The chief liaison between these two worlds is the narrator, a man who suffers from heart trouble which induces states of semi-consciousness—or "eeriness," as Carroll would call it— and trances in which he visits Outland. The other human characters in the work are subject to lesser degrees of eeriness, allowing them, too, an awareness of the Outlandish spirits. Edmund Wilson comments that "the opening railway journey, in which the narrator is dozing and mixes with the images of his dream his awareness of the lady sitting opposite him, is of an almost Joycean complexity and quite inappropriate for reading to children."[6] Florence Becker Lennon suggests that the unity of the book is achieved by the complex unity of the author: "*Sylvie and Bruno* casts more light on the author than do his masterpieces. To the reader it presents a labyrinth of neurosis, whereas to him it may have represented a healthy exercise in which he reknitted his disintegrating elements. Whatever the reason, he had great affection for the book."[7] The two worlds of *Sylvie and Bruno* clearly reflect the duality of Carroll and Dodgson, childhood innocence and responsibility, the Rectory and Oxford, Alice and the Don. Lennon observes that "the two volumes and their prefaces are an omnium—gatherum of Carroll's and Dodgson's major interests. . . . Arthur pontificates on politics, religion, art, love, science, immortality, and ruined castles; the Professor . . . instructs his learners in the use of black light and various types of glass, a megaloscope, a minifying glass, and the old-fashioned looking-glass with backward arrangement of everything from time to logic."[8] She perceives the two volumes as a "protracted figure of which the themes are the Duchess and the White Knight,"[9] the tedious little tracts and pamphlets listed under Duchess, and the charming, whimsical fancies and left-handed inventions, under White Knight. As Lennon points out, "the book could easily fly into fragments again,"[10] but the presence of the narrator, who easily and gently moves from the eerie state to the ordinary state, holds the work together.

II *Comparable to Alice Books*

In the preface to the novel Carroll states that he has attempted "to strike out yet another new path" (p. 381) and to avoid repeating the pattern of the Alice books. Nevertheless there are numerous connections between *Sylvie and Bruno* and the Alice books—and it is important to note the connections before discussing why the book "remains one of the most interesting failures in English literature."[11] The Professor, for example, has a pair of boots for horizontal weather—they are small umbrellas worn about his knees in the event that it should rain horizontally. They are clearly reminiscent of the anklets on the White Knight's horse that ward off shark bites. The Gardener waters flowers with an empty can because it is lighter to hold, an absurdity comparable to the White Knight's box for clothing and sandwiches which hung upside down to keep the rain from getting in. The Professor's Outlandish watch is related to the timepiece of the Mad Hatter. The Wonderland concept that a person who befriends Time could turn the hands of a clock and skip from breakfast to dinner develops into the Outlandish watch. In more general terms, the peculiar humor of nonsense that characterized the Alice books reasserts itself in the passages dealing with the gardener (who is always singing some nonsense verse and provides most of the poetry in the work), the Professor and the Other Professor. Furthermore, the basic contrasts between dreaming and waking states are carried over from the Alice books and emphasized to the point where technique or style practically becomes the subject. Once in Wonderland, Alice is totally enveloped in an absurd series of experiences, and one gives his attention to her sundry encounters with Wonderland creatures rather than to the fact that she is dreaming. In *Sylvie and Bruno,* on the other hand, the reader is made to concentrate upon the constant shifting realities, from the actual world, to the fairy world, back to the actual world, and the relationships between both. The psychological processes of perception are as important a part of the subject of the novel as are the two story lines. In this sense the narrator not only unifies the two worlds—the actual and the spiritual—but as the central, unifying perceiver, is the intimate subject of his own story.

Finally, the ending of *Sylvie and Bruno* is comparable to those of the Alice books. In all three works there is a crescendo that builds to a finale of contemptuous violence. Towards the end of *Alice's Adventures in Wonderland* Alice grows more assertive and finally, having reached her full size, announces: "You're nothing but a pack of cards!" Wonderland is subsequently undermined—the cards fly up in the air, and Tenniel depicts for the first time (a detail not previously noted) the various animals *without* their human characteristics. In *Sylvie and Bruno Concluded,* the Warden returns to Outland to forgive his cheating brother who usurped the throne, and Prince Bruno grows more aggressive in his contradicting the lying Sub-Warden. The scene darkens and a hurricane shakes the palace to its foundation, bursting open the windows. Through this violence the Sub-Warden is converted to honesty and he announces: "When my brother went away, you lost the best Warden you ever had. And I've been doing my best, wretched hypocrite that I am, to cheat you into making me an Emperor" (p. 688). In both works the conclusions are marked not only by violence but by transformations: characters become mere cards or animals, and an Emperor becomes a mere usurper.

III   *An Outlandish Failure*

Given the similarities between *Sylvie and Bruno* and the Alice books, why, then, is the former unsuccessful as a work of literature? The first volume sold 13,000 copies by the time of Carroll's death; the second volume was not so popular. What little success the story had in Carroll's own day was probably due to the reputation of the Alice books. The reviewers did not like it, and Carroll commented on their displeasure: "If the reviewers are right the book does not deserve to sell: if they are wrong, it will gradually get known by people recommending it to their friends."[12] In 1904 Carroll's brother Edwin attempted, with small success, to revive interest in the work by publishing an abridgement that featured only the fairy sections. In our own day the work is very inaccessible, hardly read, and usually ignored even by Carroll critics and scholars. Writing in 1937 Edmund Wilson said, "*Sylvie and Bruno*, which is never reprinted, ought to be made available."[13] Hardly a clarion call for *Sylvie and Bruno*'s resurrection, Wilson's essay does recognize the psychological complexity that makes the book interesting to the modern reader. He also notes its chief faults: "In the 'straight' parts of *Sylvie and Bruno*, Lewis Carroll was mawkishly Victorian to the point of unintentional parody."[14] In the prefaces to *Sylvie and Bruno* and its sequel one first discerns the disorder that characterizes the novel. After providing a few details about the composition of the book Carroll digresses to make moral reflections of all kinds—the need for a children's Bible, the danger of a sudden death for a person unprepared to meet his Maker, and the insincerity of elaborate church rituals. As Hudson notes, "these prefaces warn us of what is coming. The artist has not been snuffed out, but he has been overlaid by the moralist."[15] By attempting to fuse the fantasy to the conventionally uplifting didacticism of a period novel Carroll destroyed the book as a whole. The point already made with regard to Carroll's poetry applies here as well—namely, when Carroll abandons nonsense in order to write "straight," he abandons himself to outrageous sentimentality and tedious moralizing. It is

uncanny that the man who so ably handled moralizing in the
Alice books (through the Duchess, the parodies, and Alice's
own moral code) could have written the following:

"Sylvie will love all—all will love Sylvie." Bruno murmured, raising
himself on tiptoe to kiss the "little red star." "And, when you look
at it, it's gentle and blue like the sky?"
"God's own sky," Sylvie said, dreamily.
"God's own sky," the little fellow repeated, as they stood, lovingly
clinging together, and looking out into the night. "But oh, Sylvie,
what makes the sky such a *darling* blue?"
Sylvie's sweet lips shaped themselves to reply, but her voice
sounded faint and very far away. The vision was fast slipping from
my eager gaze: but it seems to me, in that last bewildering moment,
that not Sylvie but an angel was looking out through those trustful
brown eyes, and that not Sylvie's but an angel's voice was whispering
"IT IS LOVE."   (*Sylvie and Bruno Concluded*, p. 698)

Although the sentimentality, the sermonizing, and the annoy-
ing speech of Bruno (who says "oo" for "you" and "mouf" for
"mouth") seriously mar the work, one must not forget the wonderful nonsense of Mein Herr, the professors, and the mad
gardener. In order to establish a balanced estimate of the story
a brief look at some of the outlandish sections is in order.

Mein Herr, whose resemblance to the Professor suggests in
the swirl of eeriness and actuality that they are one and the
same, carries German ingenuity and inventiveness to a new
high. He explains that in his country "we have gone on select-
ing *cotton-wool*, till we have got some lighter than air! You've
no idea what a useful material it is! We call it 'Imponderal!' "
(*Sylvie and Bruno Concluded*, p. 607). The material is used
chiefly for packing articles to go by parcel post. Asked how the
postal clerk knows how much to charge for such packages, Mein
Herr replies, "That's the beauty of the new system! They pay
us: we don't pay *them*! I've often got as much as five shillings
for sending a parcel!" (p. 607).

Another project his nation developed is map making. They
began with a scale of several inches to the mile and continued
to decrease the ratio until they achieved a mile to the mile.
The narrator asks if they used such a map often and Mein Herr

explains, "It has never been spread out, yet: the farmers objected: they said it would cover the whole country, and shut out the sunlight! So we now use the country itself, as its own map, and I assure you it does nearly as well" (p. 609).

Mein Herr applies his scientific expertise even to social occasions and expounds upon four plans that have been tried in his country to stimulate conversation at social gatherings: Moving-Pictures, Wild-Creatures, Moving-Guests, and a Revolving-Humourist. The first plan involves running a small train around a circular dinner table. Each truck carries a set of pictures that pass before the guest, thereby leading him to discuss art. (With a little more ingenuity perhaps Carroll could have invented motion pictures—but apparently he was not thinking of arranging pictures in sequential order here). The second plan involved placing among the flowers on the dinner table such creatures as mice, beetles, spiders, wasps, and snakes, "so we had plenty to talk about" (p. 599). According to the third plan "we left the guests to choose their own subjects; and, to avoid monotony, we changed *them*" (p. 599). Finally, "for a *small* party we found it an excellent plan to have a round table, with a hole cut in the middle large enough to hold *one* guest. Here we placed our *best* talker. He revolved slowly, facing every guest in turn; and he told lively anecdotes the whole time!" (p. 600). The absurdity here derives from the implicit metaphor of man-as-machine or man-as-pawn that underlies these four plans.

Carroll includes in *Sylvie and Bruno Concluded* an amusing satire of the competition among English colleges for outstanding students. Mein Herr describes the scene at the railway station:

Eight of nine Heads of Colleges had assembled at the gates (no one was allowed inside), and the Station-Master had drawn a line on the pavement, and insisted on them all standing behind it. The gates were flung open! The young man darted through them, and fled like lightning down the street, while the Heads of the Colleges actually *yelled* with excitement on catching sight of him! The Proctor gave the word, in the old statutory form, "*Semel! Bis! Ter! Currite!*", and the hunt began! (pp. 615–16).

The principal of one of the colleges was shaped like a sphere, which gave him an aerodynamic advantage over his competitors.

His shape led him to investigate the theory of Accelerated Velocity. Mein Herr explains to the narrator how this principal arrived at a remarkable discovery: "the moving body, ever tending to *fall*, needs *constant support*, if it is to move in a true horizontal line. 'What, then' he asked himself, 'will give *constant support to a moving body?*' And his answer was 'Human legs!' *That* was the discovery that immortalized his name!" (p. 616). Carroll begins this entire section with a satire in the manner of Jonathan Swift and concludes it through his unique mode of nonsense.

Besides Mein Herr, the episode with the Outlandish Watch provides a pleasant interlude of nonsense amid the sensible dullness of the novel. The Professor explains how the device works: "It *goes*, of course, at the usual rate. Only the time has to go *with* it. Hence, if I move the hands, I change the time. To move them *forwards*, in *advance* of the true time, is impossible: but I can move them as much as a month *backwards*—that is the limit. And then you have the events all over again—with any alterations experience may suggest" (*Sylvie and Bruno,* p. 503). Upon moving the hands of the clock backwards the narrator is treated to witnessing a "ghostly banquet": "An empty fork is raised to the lips: there it receives a neatly-cut piece of mutton, and swiftly conveys it to the plate, where it instantly attaches itself to the mutton already there. Soon one of the plates, furnished with a complete slice of mutton and two potatoes, was handed up to the presiding gentleman, who quietly replaced the slice on the joint, and the potatoes in the dish" (p. 518). Carroll anticipates here the fun of viewing a motion picture run backwards, an event he would have applauded. Carroll it will be recalled, also played with the idea of "living backwards" in *Through The Looking-Glass.* There, however, the reversal of time was not a mere spectator sport but a curiously conscious process. The White Queen screamed, her finger bleeding, as she coolly anticipated pricking her finger on a brooch when she would fasten her shawl.

One of the most memorable nonsense characters in *Sylvie and Bruno* is the Gardener. He is the keeper of the door out of the garden in which Sylvie and Bruno occasionally find themselves. He is a vigorous, merry creature who stands on one leg while watering the flowers with an empty watering can and singing of fantastic things. A perfect singer of nonsense, the Gardener paradoxically admits "I never means nothing" (p. 418), and his songs bear him out:

> He thought he saw a Rattlesnake
> That questioned him in Greek:
> He looked again, and found it was
> The Middle of Next Week.
> "The one thing I regret," he said,
> "Is that it cannot speak!" (p. 415)

Most of his songs are set in the same meter and employ the same fantastic logic:

> He thought he saw an Elephant,
> That practised on a fife:
> He looked again, and found it was
> A letter from his wife.
> "At length I realise" he said,
> "The bitterness of Life!" (p. 408)

Amusing in themselves, the songs also reinforce the theme of dream and reality that permeates the entire story.

Phyllis Greenacre sees a relationship betwen the Gardener, Father William, and the White Knight: "all are older men, parodied, foolish inferior characters, but merry and glamorously enchanting in their unexpectedly acrobatic behavior and lilting rhythms."[16] She finds "the acrobatic, swaying, jigging, snorting rhythm" to be "a typical dream representation of sexual excitement" and that "these figures all appear as memories which are represented in dreams":

The gardener's song always comes at the point of a shift from one state to another [between dreaming and consciousness]. The repetitiveness of this excited figure and his constant association with a secret garden, the concern about whether the memory is good in the onlooker and the reciprocal questions whether the silly old fellow's brain has been injured—whether his behavior is merrily exciting or a comfort in a state of distress—would lead to the conclusion that there was some actual but repressed memory of the author's which was insistently recurring in hidden forms: that probably in his childhood Charles had been stirred at the sight of an older man, perhaps a gardener, in a state of sexual excitement.[17]

Regardless of one's attitude towards such a psychoanalytical reading of Carroll's writing, Greenacre does at least offer an explanation as to why the straight part of Carroll is so dull and conventional and the nonsense part so alive and unusual. Despite his extreme self-discipline, his dependence on orderliness, his suppression of strong emotions, his concern for accuracy and detail, a spirit of a "primitive type of 'feeling-thought'" asserts itself in his best writing and "it awakens in the reader a feeling of fantastic familiarity with an extravaganza of outlandish nonsense."[18] As some of the passages from *Sylvie and Bruno* quoted above may indicate there is little connection between them and the story of Arthur Forester and Lady Muriel Orme. The nonsense episodes in the book have a life and integrity of their own and relate to the "straight" part of the story only insofar as one is ready to accept a psychological approach to the novel— one that views, as Lennon does, the narrator as Carroll-Dodgson, a composite of the Duchess and the White Knight. Derek Hudson perhaps best summarizes what should be the modern response to the work: "*Sylvie and Bruno* bears the same relation to Lewis Carroll's earlier works, *mutatis mutandis*, as *Finnegans Wake* to the more intelligible earlier productions of James Joyce. It is worth giving time to it, though not too much, as the honourable experiment of a remarkable mind."[19]

CHAPTER 6

Man of Diverse Interests

I *Photographer*

LEWIS Carroll was one of the more visually oriented writers of his time. In contrast with an author like Charles Dickens, however, Carroll did not develop striking physical descriptions of scene and character in his writings; in fact, his prose and poetry are fairly abstract and spartan. His visual response to the world is largely isolated from his writing and relegated to his sketches, photography, and supervision of other artists' illustrations for his books. If one has a mental picture of the Mad Hatter or the White Rabbit, the odds are that it is derived from Tenniel's illustrations and not from Carroll's prose descriptions.

From childhood, when he illustrated his own magazines, through the period of *Alice's Adventures Underground*, to the last years of his life Carroll was composing sketches. He even carried sketch books with him on vacation and filled them with drawings of young girls he met by the seaside. He was constantly frustrated, however, with his inability to draw. In a letter to Gertrude Thomson, from whom he took lessons, Carroll wrote, "I *love* the effort to draw, but I utterly fail to please even my own eye—tho' now and then I seem to get somewhere *near* a right line or two, when I have a live child to draw from. But I have no time left now for such things. In the next life, I do *hope* we shall not only *see* lovely forms, such as this world does not contain, but also be able to draw them."[1] Later letters to Mrs. Thomson show him still sketching young girls from life, to within three months before his death. Despite his life-long interest in drawing, Carroll's work, when compared to that of Tenniel, Harry Furniss, and Henry Holiday, appears primitive and naive.

It was commonplace for authors to have their books illustrated

123

during the Victorian period, but it is curious to reflect that few books are so clearly remembered for their pictures as are the two Alice stories. One cannot explain this phenomenon simply by attributing the success to Tenniel—for how many people can recall other illustrations by that artist? The explanation, perhaps, lies in the perfect marriage of art and nonsense. There is more natural affinity between the two than there is between art and literature, where there is usually a rivalry. In reading a novel such as *Middlemarch*, one might be displeased with a drawing of Dorothea Brook, for her psychological complexity and ambiguity would be threatened by the fixed physical representation of her. It is precisely because nonsense eschews ambiguity, as Sewell has observed, that the illustrations are so effective: "The providing of pictures is a regular part of the Nonsense game. They sterilize the mind's powers of invention and combination of images while seeming to nourish it, and by precision and detail they contribute towards detachment and definition of the elements of the Nonsense universe."[2] The characters in Wonderland, for example, do not have a psychological reality; they are, for the most part, mindless. Their existence is comprised solely of their nonsense statements (which do not seem to arise from any intelligible core of being) and their physical appearance as delineated in the precise illustrations.

Phyllis Greenacre comments on the visual aspect of Carroll's work in terms of his psychology: "The spirit of both *Alice* books is that of an unplanned sight-seeing trip through a marvelously strange country. The title, *Alice's Adventures in Wonderland* in the one instance, and the entrance through the *Looking Glass* into an extraordinary country in the other, re-emphasize the voyeuristic theme."[3] In *The Hunting of the Snark,* the Baker is punished by annihilation in the act of seeing the Boojum. Greenacre explains the Boojum as "some representation of the primal scene, in which the sexual images of the parents are fused into a frightening or awe-inspiring single figure" and sees the last "fit" as "an acting out of the primal scene with the Baker first standing 'erect and sublime' and then plunging into the chasm between the crags."[4]

One of the most satisfying outlets for Carroll's interest in looking came in photography. What began as a hobby in 1856 became a passionate devotion for nearly twenty four years. During that period Carroll developed into one of the most skillful portrait photographers of his day. He did his own developing and printing at a time when this was an exceedingly complicated and exacting job. Photography had only become available to the public a few years before Carroll took it up. He was now able to approach his favorite subject, the beautiful girl child, in a new and exciting way. Like the Butcher in the *Snark* who "thought of his childhood, left far far behind— / That blissful and innocent state," Carroll throughout his life looked back on his childhood with nostalgia. Now, through photography, he could freeze images of youthful innocence through countless photographs of young girls.

Although he frequently sought out eminent men and women to photograph—such as Dante Gabriel Rossetti, Ellen Terry, and Alfred Tennyson—he achieved greater artistic interest, according to Helmut Gernsheim, in his pictures of children.[5] He was simply more relaxed in the company of children and could work with them more effectively as subjects. He owned a large variety of costumes, many of which were from the Drury Lane pantomimes, and he dressed up the little girls as Chinese, Cinderellas, parlor maids, beggar maids, and Little Red Riding-Hoods. The majority of his girl sitters were the daughters of clergymen, of Oxford professors, and of well-known writers and artists. There was a snobbish streak in Carroll that made it impossible for him to photograph real beggar maids. In a letter to Beatrice Hatch he wrote that "below a certain line, it is hardly wise to let a girl have a 'gentleman' friend," though he does say that some of his little friends "are of a *rather* lower status than myself."[6] Gernsheim condemns the costume pictures for their lamentable concession to Victorian taste but as a photographer of unadorned children he feels that Carroll "achieves an excellence which in its way can find no peer."[7] Carroll considered children's simple nightdresses most attractive and had a number of little girls pose in them. He once wrote to a mother, "If they have such things as flannel night-gowns, that makes as pretty a dress as you can desire. White does pretty well, but nothing like flannel."[8] The texture and color of flannel made it more photogenic and enhanced the naturalness of the child. In a letter to Harry Furniss, the illustrator of *Sylvie and Bruno,* about dresses for the fairy children Carroll goes a step beyond nightdresses: "I wish I dared dispense with *all* costume. Naked children are so perfectly pure and lovely: but Mrs. Grundy would be furious—it would never do." But he carefully discriminated between naked boys and naked girls: "I confess I do *not* admire naked boys. They always seem to need clothes—whereas one hardly sees why the lovely forms of girls should *ever* be covered up."[9] Carroll took great pains, however, to avoid ever offending the propriety of either parents or children. He wrote that "If I had the loveliest child in the world, to draw or photograph, and found she had a modest shrinking (however slight, and however easily overcome / from being taken nude, I should feel it was a solemn duty owed to God to drop the request altogether."[10] Apparently his models did not always shrink from such requests, for Carroll did make a number of photographs of nude girls. None has survived for publication because he stipulated that after his death they should be returned to the sitters or their parents, or else be destroyed.

Carroll's interest in photography is inextricably related to his interest in young girls. It is through the elaborate and socially acceptable ritual of photographing his youthful subjects that he apparently derived so much satisfaction, the ritual (and the camera) always providing a comfortable esthetic distance. He was constantly on the lookout for new little girls to photograph. In his diary he records, for example, that a Mrs. Colonel Franklin's "little girl was one I observed at the school-feast and had enquired her name, with a view to getting Mrs. Cameron to photograph her for me."[11] Later, he writes, "I was lounging about on the beach, and came on the same little unknown child—such a little gypsy beauty, rich brown complexion and black eyes."[12] Finally, several days later, he managed to photograph the girl himself. A diary entry for March 1863 reveals a list of 107 names of girls "photographed or to be photographed."[13] In 1877 he saw a girl named Connie Gilchrist playing a part in a children's pantomime and noted in his diary that she was "one of the most beautiful children, in face and figure, that I have ever seen. I must get an opportunity of photographing her." About three months later he got to meet her and wrote, "I was decidedly pleased with Connie, who has a refined and modest manner, with just a touch of shyness, and who is about the most gloriously beautiful child (both face and figure) that I ever saw. One would like to do 100 photographs of her."[14] One could cite scores of similar entries throughout the quarter of a century that Carroll tirelessly pursued his photography. It is noteworthy that many of these entries reveal that his first response to seeing a young girl is a desire to photograph her—not talk to her, take her somewhere, play with her, hold her, or any of a number of other possible responses. It was careful and intense observation of the mysterious Franklin girl that led Carroll to want to photograph her—his mental picture of her apparently never satisfactory until he got it aligned through the camera lens and fixed on the film.

"The main charm of photography for his artist soul," writes Lennon, "was its difficulty."[15] When photography became simplified by the invention of the convenient dry plate process, he abandoned the art. Over the years Carroll's manner of living, like his photography, became strictly patterned. From finding new sitters to pasting the finished photograph in his album, Carroll transformed a hobby into an elaborate ritual—and the idea of replacing the complex wet plate process for a new and easy method must have threatened the entire ritual.

Many of Carroll's photographs were taken in Oxford, at the Deanery, Christ Church, in his rooms, and at a hired studio. When, in 1868, he moved into a suite of rooms in Tom Quad he had erected on the flat college roof a photographic glasshouse. It was to this magical room that numerous children climbed in order to be transformed into Turks, parlor maids, and fisherboys. One of his sitters later recalled the experience:

Perhaps the most vivid memories of the Oxford children are connected with the great experience of being photographed. How well they can remember climbing up the dark oak staircase leading out of Tom Quad to the studio of the top floor of his rooms! The smell of certain chemicals will still bring back a vision of the mysterious dark cupboard where he developed his plates, of the dressing-room where strange costumes had to be donned, and of the rather awe-inspiring ceremony of being posed, with fastidious care, as

Turk, Chinaman, fisher-boy, or in a group with several others to form a picture.[16]

Having secured a desirable sitter (oftentimes obtained only after much correspondence, meeting friends of friends who have an attractive daughter, wrangling invitations, etc.) and having set up the elaborate equipment of the glass house, Carroll could proceed with the final stages of the photographic ritual. He had created in his rooms a paradise for children, the atmosphere of which would help bring them to just the right mood to be photographed. There was an array of dolls and toys, a distorting mirror, a clockwork bear, a flying bat which he made, a collection of music boxes, and an organette that played perforated sheet music. When they grew tired of these amusements Carroll would sit a child on his knee and tell her fascinating stories, illustrating them with humorous drawings on scraps of paper. When she seemed thoroughly elated by the procedures he would pose her for a photograph before the appropriate mood had passed. Sometimes he would allow the children to go into the darkroom and watch him develop the large glass plates.

Without casting a sinister light upon Carroll's relationship with his sitters, one may nevertheless note the compelling parallel between his photographic adventures and the sexual adventures of a typical bachelor (which Carroll obviously was not). Both keep an eye out for attractive girls, strategically work out meetings, establish a proper atmosphere of entertainment and relaxation that serves as a kind of foreplay, and then proceed to the crucial moment of possession. Even Carroll's list of 107 names of girls "photographed or to be photographed" fits into this pattern of seduction and possession. Considering the likelihood that he never loved any woman in an adult fashion, it is not surprising that he should adopt the conventional procedures of the bachelor on the make for dealing with little girls who, after all, in Carroll's own words, comprised three-fourths of his life.

II *Wizard of Math and Logic*

According to Warren Weaver Lewis Carroll was a rather ordinary mathematician. As a lecturer in Christ Church and as a tutor, he was concerned with elementary aspects of mathematics— arithmetic, algebra, trigonometry, plane and solid geometry, and less sophisticated portions of calculus and differential equations. Despite his devotion to math, however, his interest "was never coupled to a deep knowledge or a large natural talent." "Formal logic," Weaver contends, "is the one subject to which Dodgson can be said to have made any real contribution."[17] Logic, however, he obviously considered to be a game, an attitude expressed in the title of his first book on the subject, *The Game of Logic.* As with his writing, his mathematics, when it stays on the orthodox side of Wonderland, is elementary and dull—but when his reckless and elusive madness takes charge both his writing and mathematics come alive.

As John Fisher has noted, Carroll possessed "a magician's instinct for tracking down the impossible," and "was able to supply something more than the straightforward academic approach to his studies in mathematics and logic."[18] His interest in baffling and mystifying others could be realized through the infinite means of these two fields of study. Ideas for games, puzzles, and riddles occupied his mind at all hours, and he recorded them in his books and essays throughout his life. John Fisher has collected many of these conundrums into one volume, entitled *The Magic of Lewis Carroll.* Games are games and most of them are not worth discussing here, for they have an anonymous sort of quality. There are, however, several examples that have the distinctive literary flavor of his nonsense books.

Dynamics of a parti-cle, a small pamphlet of political satire published in 1865, contains some interesting mathematical puns:

1. PLAIN SUPERFICIALITY is the character of a speech, in which any two points being taken, the speaker is found to lie wholly with regard to those two points.
2. PLAIN ANGER is the inclination of two voters to one another, who meet together, but whose views are not in the same direction
3. When a Proctor, meeting another Proctor, makes the votes on one side equal to those on the other, the feeling entertained by each side is called RIGHT ANGER.
4. When two parties, coming together, feel a Right Anger, each is *said* to be COMPLEMENTARY to the other (though, strictly speaking, this is very seldom the case).
5. OBTUSE ANGER is that which is greater than Right Anger.[19]

The Offer of the Clarendon Trustees, published in 1868, proposes a number of additions at Oxford that would accommodate students in their mathematical calculations:

A. A very large room for calculating Greatest Common Measure. To this a small one might be attached for Least Common Multiple: this, however, might be dispensed with.
B. A piece of open ground for keeping Roots and practising their extraction: it would be advisable to keep Square Roots by themselves, as their corners are apt to damage others.
C. A room for reducing Fractions to their Lowest Terms. This should be provided with a cellar for keeping the Lowest Terms when found, which might also be available to the general body of undergraduates, for the purpose of "Keeping Terms."
D. A large room, which might be darkened, and fitted up with a magic lantern, for the purpose of exhibiting Circulating Decimals in the act of circulation. This might also contain cupboards, fitted with glass-doors, for keeping the various Scales of Notation.
E. A narrow strip of ground, railed off and carefully leveled, for investigating the properties of Asymptotes, and testing practically whether Parallel Lines meet or not: for this purpose it should reach, to use the expressive language of Euclid, "ever so far."
      This last process, of "continually producing The Lines," may require centuries or more: but such a period, though long in the life of an individual, is nothing in the life of the University.[20]

Euclid and his Modern Rivals further illustrates Carroll's fusion of mathematics with literary whimsy, a union clearly relevant to *Through the Looking Glass.* Carroll's purpose in writing this book was to demonstrate that with only very slight changes Euclid is the best geometry book on the market. The form of his argument, however, is that of a five-act comedy. The opening scene presents the Mathematical Lecturer in the guise of Minos, talking to himself as he grades examination papers:

So, my friend! That's the way you prove I. 19, is it? Assuming I. 20? Cool, refreshingly cool! But stop a bit! Perhaps he doesn't 'declare to win' on Euclid. Let's see. Ah, just so! 'Legendre,' of course! Well, I suppose I must give him full marks for it: what's the question worth?—Wait a bit, though! Where's his paper of yesterday? I've a very decided impression he was all for 'Euclid' then: and I know the paper had I. 20, on it . . . Ah, here it is! 'I think we know the sweet Roman hand.' Here's the proposition, as large as life, and proved by I. 19. 'Now, infidel, I have thee on the hip!' You shall have such a sweet thing to do in *viva-voce*, my very dear friend! You shall have the two propositions together and take them in any order you like. It's my profound conviction that you don't know how to prove either of them without the other. They'll have to introduce each other, like Messrs. Pyke and Pluck. But what a fearful confusion the whole subject is getting into![21]

The human or literary element that generates the "fearful confusion" is the life-giving force of this book, for it is constantly at war with the rigidity of a pure mathematical system. This is essentially the same battle that was waged by the supple, fallible Alice in a world of unyielding rules of logic and games.

In Scene ii, Minos sets out to review modern geometries without the aid of Euclid:

Min.: It will be weary work to do it all alone. And yet, I suppose you cannot, even with *your* supernatural powers, fetch me the authors themselves?

Euc.: I dare not. The living human race is so strangely prejudiced. There is nothing men object to so emphatically as being transferred by ghosts from place to place. I cannot say they are consistent in this matter: they are forever 'raising' or 'laying' us poor ghosts—we cannot even haunt a garret without having the parish at our heels, bent on making us change our quarters: whereas if *I* were to venture to move one single boy—say to lift him by the hair of his head over only two or three houses, and to set him down safe and sound in a neighbour's garden—why, I give you my word, it would be the talk of the town for the next month![22]

Ghosts and the supernatural in a book on geometry! Euclid could as easily appear in *Phantasmagoria* or *Sylvie and Bruno*. His proposed elevation of the boy is comparable to Alice's lifting the White King to the table.

In Act II the reader is introduced to Herr Niemand (nobody) in a manner clearly suggestive of the Cheshire Cat's entrance, grin first: "Minos sleeping: To him enter, first a cloud of tobacco-smoke, secondly the bowl, and thirdly the stem of a gigantic meerschaum; fourthly the phantasm of Herr Niemand, carrying a pile of phantom-books, the works of Euclid's Modern Rivals, phantastically bound."[23]

Before going on to a difficult discussion of a system of codifying the various methods of treating parallel lines, Carroll treats his reader to a madcap satire of the Association for the Improvement of Geometrical Teaching:

Enter a phantasmic procession, grouped about a banner, on which is emblazoned in letters of gold the title 'Association for the Improvement of Things in General.' Foremost in the line marches Nero, carrying his unfinished 'Scheme for the Amelioration of Rome': while among the crowd which follows him may be noticed—Guy Fawkes, President of the 'Association for raising the position of Members of Parliament'—The Marchioness de Brinvilliers, Foundress of the 'Association for the Amendment of the Digestive Faculty'—and The Rev. F. Gustrell (the being who cut down Shakespeare's mulberry-tree) leader of the 'Association for the Refinement of Literary Taste.' Afterwards enter, on the other side, Sir Isaac Newton's little dog, 'Diamond,' carrying in his mouth a half-burnt roll of manuscript. He pointedly avoids the procession and the banner, and marches past alone, serene in the consciousness that he, single-pawed, conceived and carried out his great 'Scheme for the Advancement of Mathematical Research', without the aid of any association whatever.[24]

The playfulness exhibited in Carroll's mathematical writings is even more forcefully apparent in his two small works on logic, *The Game of Logic and Symbolic Logic, Part I.* R. B. Braithwaite has observed that "Carroll regarded formal and symbolic logic not as a systematic knowledge about valid thought nor yet as an art for teaching a person to think correctly, but as a game."[25] Carroll's procedure in *The Game of Logic* is to present not a series of facts, but a series of agreements for the reader to enter into. He proposes certain "universes" that contain all members of a certain class. Thus, there might be a "Universe of Cakes," a "Universe of Hornets," or a "Universe of Dragons." With regard to the latter, Carroll declares: "Remember, I don't guarantee the Premises to be *facts*. In the first place, I never even saw a Dragon: and, in the second place.

it isn't of the slightest consequence to us, as *Logicians,* whether our Premises are true or false: all *we* have to make out is whether they *lead logically to the Conclusion,* so that, if *they* were true, *it* would be true also."[26] In *Symbolic Logic,* Carroll takes his argument a step further: "I maintain that every writer may adopt his own rule, provided of course that it is consistent with itself and with the accepted facts of logic."[27] As he already noted, the accepted facts of logic vary according to logician. There is a clear relationship between the artificial and arbitrary system of logic advocated by Carroll in his books on logic and the closed system of play in such works as *The Hunting of the Snark.* The famous "Rule of Three," for example, is entirely consistent with Carroll's observations about premises and the adoption of one's own rule. The Bellman practiced what Carroll preached.

Carroll the mathematician and logician, then, is inseparable from Carroll the nonsense writer: the principles of order and play hold the same for both. Braithwaite points out that nearly all of Carroll's jokes are jokes either in pure or applied logic: "When a child has learned that a form of words is used in one particular context, he is surprised to find that it cannot be used in some other context; and the attractiveness of Carroll lies in the fact that his use of a phrase in an apparently correct but really nonsensical way appears as plausible to him as to the child." Braithwaite goes on to discuss the logic of Carroll's puns and paradoxes, and concludes his essay by noting Humpty Dumpty to be "the masterpiece of Lewis Carroll as unconscious logician."[28] Listening to Humpty's statement, "When *I* use a word, it means just what I choose it to mean—neither more nor less," one realizes he is actually in the presence of a very *conscious* logician. In *Symbolic Logic,* Carroll not only granted permission to every writer to "adopt his own rule," but maintained that "any writer of a book is fully authorised in attaching any meaning he likes to any word or phrase he intends to use."[29] Humpty Dumpty's definition of glory as "a nice knock-down argument" is thus notably defended, a defense that serves as an important reminder that Lewis Carroll and Charles Dodgson are one and the same person.

III *Miscellaneous Essays*

In the haven of Tom Quad, immersed in a world of mathematics, logic, nonsense, and children, Carroll spent little time worrying or writing about the great social and economic problems of his day. Occasionally, however, something would trigger a strong response from him as when, in 1875, a letter appeared in *The Spectator* on the subject of vivisection. A week later Carroll published a long letter in *The Pall Mall Gazette*. "Vivisection as a Sign of the Times" uses the subject of vivisection as a spring board to attack the new secular education made possible by the Education Act of 1870: "How far may vivisection be regarded as a sign of the times, and a fair specimen of that higher civilization which a purely secular State education is to give us?" He flatly rejects the logic that suggests that a nation's moral conduct will be improved through scientific education. Carroll himself had taken up the study of anatomy in 1872 after helplessly watching a man in convulsions, which may have led him to ask, "Can the man who has once realized by minute study what the nerves are, what the brain is, and what waves of agony one can convey to the other, go forth and wantonly inflict pain on any sentient being?" He comes to the conclusion that secular education without religious or moral training not only diminishes one's moral growth but actually encourages selfishness: "The world has seen and tired of the worship of Nature, of Reason, of Humanity; for this nineteenth century has been reserved the development of the most refined religion of all—the worship of Self." Selfishness is the keynote of all secular education and vivisection is "a glaring, a wholly unmistakable case in point." The nineteenth century will thus foster the unprincipled man of science who, "looking forth over a world which will then own no other sway than his, shall exult in the thought that he has made of this fair green earth, if not a heaven for man, at least a hell for animals."[30]

Four months after he published the preceding letter he wrote an article entitled "Some Popular Fallacies about Vivisection" for *The Fortnightly Review*. After considering man's right only to inflict a painless death upon an animal, Carroll proceeds to distinguish between killing for food and killing for knowledge. He contends that the effect of vivisection is more damaging to the scientist than to the animal: "The hapless animal suffers, dies, 'and there is an end': but the man whose sympathies have been deadened, and whose selfishness has been fostered, by the contemplation of pain deliberately inflicted, may be the parent of others equally brutalized, and so bequeath a curse to future ages." In this connection one may recall that the Baker, Carroll's most notorious hunter, was destroyed by the hunt. Carroll's thirteenth fallacy, however, is the most horrifying (and prophetic of all): "*That the practise of vivisection will never be extended so as to include human subjects.*" He sees the day coming "when anatomy can claim as legitimate subject for experiment, first, our condemned criminals—next, perhaps, the inmates of our refuges for incurables—then the hopeless lunatic, the pauper hospital-patient, and generally 'him that hath no helper.' "[31]

Viewing a sound education in the liberal arts as the basis for a sane and humane society, Carroll's "Natural Science at Oxford," published in *The Pall Mall Gazette*, attacks the new emphasis upon science in the university curriculum. Almost crotchety in his conservatism, he complains that Latin and Greek may both vanish from the curriculum and that logic, philosophy, and history may follow. He fears the day when Oxford falls into the hands of those whose only education has been in science. This view is part of the more general issues of the time, especially the concern over the lack of morality in a scientific education. He also laments the decay of English language evident in much scientific writing. Having corrected some pages of the *Anthropological Review* for the press, he exclaims that he has never read "even in the 'local news' of a country paper, such slipshod, such deplorable English." As a general principle he argues that the exclusive study of any *one* subject does not really quite educate a person: "therefore it is that I seek to rouse an interest, beyond the limits of Oxford, in preserving classics as an essential feature of a University education."[32] This essay, taken with the two on vivisection, sets forth an argument similar to John Henry Newman's in *The Idea of a University*. Newman had argued that "to give undue prominence to one [branch of knowledge] is to be unjust to another,"[33] and, of course, demanded the inclusion of religion and morality in his idea of the liberal arts.

Carroll's essay "Feeding the Mind" arose out of an illness he experienced in July of 1883. He diagnosed his malady as "a sort of ague, with cystitis" and noted that he suffered "two miserable feverish nights, in a state between waking and sleeping, and worrying over the same idea (something about Common Room ledgers) over and over again."[34] During this period he spent many hours lying on his sofa reading novels. This experience led him to see that the mind must be trained and nourished no less than the body—for never before did he abandon himself so completely to the reading of fiction.

"Feeding the Mind" was originally planned as a lecture that Carroll delivered for W. H. Draper, Vicar of Alfreton, in September of 1884. Although Carroll suffered another attack of feverish ague while he was at Alfreton, he nevertheless dutifully delivered his promised lecture. The Rev. Draper noted Carroll's "nervous, highly strung manner as he stood before the little room full of simple people"[35] to speak on the importance of feeding the mind. A delightful talk, characteristic of Carroll's whimsy, it was not published until 1907.

The metaphor of food, which unifies the essay, was probably suggested to Carroll by Francis Bacon's essay "On Studies," in which Bacon argued that some books are to be tasted, others to be chewed, and still others to be swallowed and digested. Carroll imagines a dialogue that might ensue were one able to take his mind to be examined by a physician:

"Why, what have you been doing with this mind lately? How have you fed it? It looks pale, and the pulse is very slow."

"Well, doctor, it has not had much regular food lately. I gave it a lot of sugar-plums yesterday."

"Sugar-plums! What kind?"

"Well, they were a parcel of conundrums, sir."

"Ah, I thought so. Now just mind this: if you go on playing tricks like that, you'll spoil all its teeth, and get laid up with mental indigestion. You must have nothing but the plainest reading for the next few days. Take care now! No novels on any account!"[36]

One is clearly reminded in this passage of Carroll's illness and his subsequent indulgence in novel reading. It was not atypical of a Victorian gentleman, especially one reared in a religious household, to consider the reading of novels as a frivolous, if not sinful, activity. There is no indication that Carroll considered novels to be serious works of art. His own reading was usually carefully balanced: novels were a mere spice to a diet of mathematical, logical, technical, and theological writings. He goes on to say that the effects of reading "the unwholesome novel" are "low spirits, unwillingness to work, weariness of existence—in fact . . . mental nightmare."[37] He makes novel reading sound as detrimental as lotus eating.

This Calvinistic turn of mind is further demonstrated by his belief that the mind should be nimble, athletic (not unlike the disciplined bodies of the young boys in Arnold's Rugby School). He ponders the idea of mental gluttony: "I wonder if there is such a thing in nature as a FAT MIND? I really think I have met with one or two: minds which could not keep up with the slowest trot in conversation; could not jump over a logical fence, to save their lives; always got stuck fast in a narrow argument; and, in short, were fit for nothing but to waddle helplessly through the world."[38] Carroll's body, like his mind, was trim and nimble throughout his life, and he obviously views fat minds, like fat people, as self-indulgent and comical.

Finally, one can see from this essay Carroll's compulsive orderliness as he ridicules the thoroughly well-read man who cannot organize his learning well enough to respond to simple questions: "all this for want of making up his knowledge into proper bundles and ticketing them."[39] One is pleased to remember that the Baker, in *The Hunting of the Snark*, "had forty-two boxes, all carefully packed, / With his name painted clearly on each: / But, since he omitted to mention the fact, / They were all left behind on the beach." And so, it seems, even a well-fed, orderly mind like the Baker's is only an asset insofar as it does not exhibit the classical professorial malady of comedy, absent-mindedness.

CHAPTER 7

Conclusion

I The Critics

*A*LICE'S *Adventures in Wonderland* is one of the world's most translated books, and Carroll is one of the world's most quoted authors. The characters he created have lived in the imaginations of his audience to an extent unattained by any other writer save Shakespeare, Dickens, and Conan Doyle. This vast popularity of his works has made the role of the critic a difficult one. There has been and still is a feeling that any serious evaluation of Alice and her friends is inherently ridiculous and results in an unintentional parody of criticism and scholarship. This attitude is clearly expressed in John Fisher's recent edition of Carroll's puzzles, *The Magic of Lewis Carroll* (1973):

This volume has been an attempt to bring forward some of the magic and fun of Lewis Carroll smothered by the spate of serious criticism and analysis of the author that has gushed forth in recent years. Academics, often earnestly seizing upon the *Alice* books as a coat-hanger for their own fantasies, have variously interpreted Carroll's representation of Alice Liddell as pastoral swain and phallic symbol, as Jungian anima and the first acid-head in children's literature; have laid bare the books themselves as allegories of philosophical systems and Darwinian evolution, of the Oxford Movement and Victorian toilet training.[1]

It is precisely this anti-intellectual attitude that led Edmund Wilson, in 1932, to write: "If the Lewis Carroll centenary has produced anything of special interest, I have failed to see it. C. L. Dodgson was a most interesting man and deserves better of his admirers, who revel in his delightfulness and cuteness but do not give him any serious attention."[2] Since 1932 Carroll has received volumes of serious critical attention, some of it bril-

138

liant, some of it bad. It is certainly debatable to argue that "the spate of serious criticism" has "smothered" the fun of Carroll's writings. Fun is an intellectual as well as an imaginative exercise, as exemplified by the very puzzles and riddles Mr. Fisher has collected. It is fun to view Alice from the pastoral perspective of William Empson, and it is fun to think with Phyllis Greenacre that Carroll's identification with his mother precludes the strong, active, and well-respected adult male figure from his writings. And it is fun to read Carroll from the point of view of Elizabeth Sewell who contends that nonsense is a sophisticated linguistic game that creates a self-contained, orderly universe. Not all of the critical approaches are compatible, but most of them provide insights and explanations that enrich one's reading of the works themselves. Carroll's books have come of critical age and the public no longer needs the paternalistic defense of the fun hucksters who view Freud and Jung, allegorists and formalists, biographers and psychoanalysts as dangerous enemies of enjoyment. Samuel Johnson and G. Wilson Knight have not diminished the comic stature of Falstaff anymore than William Empson and Phyllis Greenacre have tarnished the joys of Wonderland.

The danger in Carrollian, as in all criticism, is the possessive spirit of the critic who would offer a definitive reading or interpretation. The early allegorical interpretations of *The Hunting of The Snark*, for example, if accepted, preclude any other reading and thereby diminish the depth of the work while failing to explain why readers enjoyed it before the "explanation" was provided. Even the eclectic critic, therefore, must reject such rigid and closed readings as esthetically damaging and intellectually untenable. One must boldly assert that the Snark is not the atomic bomb, that the Boojum is not a symbol of a business slump, and that the whole poem is not an anti-vivisectionist tract. With other critical approaches, however, one must be simply tentative.

The psychoanalytical readings of the *Alice* books do not purport to exhaust their "meaning" but to explain why some things appear there as they do. To view the sea of tears in which Alice swims as the amniotic fluid bathing the fetus is not to preclude seeing it as Lethe. Alice can be the anima, the genteel

Victorian child, the swain, and the eternal ingenue. Although some of the Freudian critics disclose a psychological allegory (girl-phallus, rabbit hole-vagina), they are primarily concerned with the Alice books as products of the author's subconscious mind, and are thereby a different breed from the critics who impose a rigid conscious allegory upon the works. Anyone who is amused with Humpty Dumpty's ability to interpret "all the poems that ever were invented—and a good many that haven't been invented just yet" ought to welcome and relish "the spate of serious criticism" that has "gushed forth." It is a clear sign that Alice is alive and well. Here is what Carroll himself, writing about *The Hunting of the Snark*, had to say on the subject. "Still, you know, words mean more than we mean to express when we use them; so a whole book ought to mean a great deal more than the writer means. So whatever good meanings are in the book, I'm glad to accept as the meaning of the book."[3]

II   *Alice's Survival*

Alice is no more the property of the critics than she is of Lewis Carroll. She has been adopted and adapted by all people in practically every country of the world. Alice and the other characters of Wonderland and Looking-Glass Land have appeared on biscuit tins, playing cards, and greeting cards, have been shaped into glass and silver figurines, and have shown up in puppet shows, professional stage plays, motion pictures, and television. Carroll himself encouraged the popularization of the Alice stories by granting permission for several stage performances based upon *Alice's Adventures in Wonderland* as well as for an operetta by Savile Clarke in 1886. Afraid of exploitation of his success, he wrote to Macmillan asking that the two Alice books be copied out in dramatic form and be duly registered as two dramas. Over the years, however, he discovered that he had little legal control over adaptations as Alice quickly became available to an ever increasing audience. In 1898 the *Pall Mall Gazette* took a survey of the popularity of children's books, and *Alice's Adventures in Wonderland* led them all. In our own day the Alice stories are available in countless children's versions, not to mention the many paperback editions of the complete tales. In 1933 Paramount produced a version of *Wonderland* with W. C. Fields as Humpty Dumpty, Cary Grant as the Mock Turtle, and Gary Cooper as the White Knight, and in 1951 Walt Disney's animated version made its disappointing appearance. In both the redrawing and retelling of the original, Disney produced a sentimental adaptation. Jonathan Miller's production surpasses the earlier ones and features *Punch* editor Malcolm Muggeridge as the Gryphon, Sir Michael Redgrave as the Caterpillar, and Peter Sellers as the King of Hearts. Among the notable dramatic adaptations of *Wonderland* are those by Eva le Gallienne and Florida Friebus at the Civic Repertory Theatre in 1932, by Clemence Dane in 1943 at the Scala Theatre in London, and Andre Gregory's *Alice* in 1970, in New York. Edward Albee's *Tiny Alice*, 1964, is also indebted to Carroll. There have also been several musical renditions, including an Afro-American soul musical in New York, and, of course, Deems Taylor's *Through the Looking-Glass.*

Alice and her associates have also been variously shaped by several illustrators: Carroll himself, of course, Tenniel, Mabel Lucie Attwell, Peter Newell, Arthur Rackham, Charles Robinson, Thomas Maybank, Harry Furniss, Fritz Kredel, and Salvador Dali, to name just a few, have all attempted to capture the pictorial essence of Alice and company. Tenniel's drawings, however, have never been surpassed, are indelibly associated with the text, and have strongly influenced subsequent illustrators.

The Alice books have provided the world with an inexhaustible fairy tale. There are simply too many aspects of Alice for them ever to be finally illustrated or explicated. In his art Carroll has achieved a purity that, in the words of Edmund Wilson, "is almost unique in a period so cluttered and cumbered, in which even the preachers of doom to the reign of materialism bore the stamp and stain of the industrial system in the hard insistence of their sentences and in the turbidity of their belchings of rhetoric. They have shrunk now, but *Alice* still stands."[4]

III   *The Legacy of Play*

Although Carroll is primarily remembered for the enormous success and unique artistry of the Alice books, his other works have also proven to be of lasting value. *The Hunting of the*

Snark, Euclid and His Modern Rivals, Rhyme? and Reason?, A Tangled Tale, The Game of Logic, Sylvie and Bruno, Sylvie and Bruno Concluded, Symbolic Logic, and *Three Sunsets and Other Poems* display an extraordinary intelligence and creativity. Each of these volumes, like the Alice books, affirms a similar thesis: the inestimable value of play, an activity that releases man from mechanical routine and enhances his human spirit. In a letter to one of his child friends Carroll wrote: "Do you ever play at games? Or is your idea of life 'breakfast, lessons, dinner, lessons, tea, lessons, bed, lessons, breakfast, lessons,' and so on? It is a very neat plan of life and almost as interesting as being a sewing machine or a coffee grinder."[5] Games, like laughter, remind us of our humanity in so far as they free us of mechanical routine. Logic, to Carroll, is essentially a game. Euclid is a comic character in a drama (*Euclid and His Modern Rivals*) as well as a propounder of axioms. The Snark hunters are involved in an elaborate hunt which entails the observance of the rules and regulations of a game. Kathleen Blake, in *Play, Games and Sport: The Literary Works of Lewis Carroll* (Ithaca and London: Cornell University Press, 1974), demonstrates that the idea of play is central to all of Carroll's writings. The view of life as a game is essentially a comic (not frivolous) one and such a view, with its focus upon spontaneity and disinterestedness, arouses and engages our human instincts. As Donald J. Gray observed, when Carroll brought together his intellect and playfulness "he made structures so complex and entire that, for whatever reason we come to them, and whatever we take from them, we can be held within them simply by the pleasure of watching Dodgson playing, this time, with the stuff of his very life, and at the very top of his game."[6]

Behind all of the writings is his sense of life as an enormous puzzle, one to be worked at to the end, and one never completely to be solved. Writing to his brother Skeffington, who invited him to preach a sermon in Worcester (in 1893), Carroll said: "I am glad to take opportunities of saying 'words for God,' which one *hopes* may prove of some use to somebody. I always feel that a sermon is worth the preaching, if it has given *some* help to even *one* soul in the puzzle of life."[7] Judith Bloomingdale's view of Carroll reinforces this idea: "As Jung has also stated, the man possessed by the *anima* sees all of life as a game or puzzle. This perception seems to be the missing link between the two personalities of Charles Dodgson and Lewis Carroll."[8] It is little wonder, then, that such men as Ludwig Wittgenstein and James Joyce were drawn to Carroll's writings, for in them they discovered a sophisticated play with language and an attempt to create a self-contained world of words, an attempt that would distil the essence of civilized play and human understanding. If the puzzle of life could not be solved, at least one could create his own universe, complex but regulated, puzzling but rational. Joyce has thus appropriately addressed Carroll in *Finnegans Wake* as "Dodgfather, Dodgson and Coo,"[9] Dodgson as Father, Son, and Holy Spirit.

"The Wasp in a Wig" Episode from Through the Looking Glass

IN 1974 Sotheby Parke Bernet and Company, a London auctioneering firm, listed the following item: "Dodgson (C. L.) 'Lewis Carroll.' Galley proofs for a suppressed portion of 'Through the Looking-Glass.'" Until 1974 the suppressed episode was believed by Carroll scholars to have been lost. After Carroll's death in 1898 an unknown person purchased the galleys and nothing is known of their history until Sotheby auctioned them. Norman Armour, Jr., of New York City, now owns the galleys and permitted the Lewis Carroll Society of North America to publish them in August 1977, edited by Martin Gardner. Edward Guiliano, the editor of *Carroll Studies*, has kindly sent me the uncorrected galley proof of the Lewis Carroll Society's edition of "The Wasp in a Wig," including Gardner's preface, introduction, and notes, so that I could supply this brief appendix.

"The Wasp in a Wig" was suppressed because Carroll's illustrator, John Tenniel, refused to work with it. "Don't think me brutal," he wrote to Carroll, "but I am bound to say that the '*wasp*' chapter doesn't interest me in the least, I can't see my way to a picture." Considering the weird creatures that Tenniel did draw for Carroll's books, it seems odd that he rejected a wasp in a wig as being "beyond the appliances of art." In any event, Carroll suppressed the episode in galley stage but fortunately preserved the galleys.

"The Wasp in a Wig," according to Gardner and Guiliano, is not a separate chapter of *Through the Looking-Glass* but a portion of the chapter on the White Knight. The Wasp represents a bad-tempered, lower-class laborer in his declining years. Alice responds to his cross remarks with incredible patience and kindness. In Gardner's words, "it is an episode in which extreme youth confronts extreme age." Furthermore, it is an episode in which the proper breeding and speech of the middle class confront the rudeness and slang of the lower class. The passage exhibits the tone, word play, and humorous nonsense characteristic of the rest of the book, but the fact that it repeats many of the themes that occur elsewhere weakens its artistic merit.

The following passage will serve to illustrate the quality of the humor, which in this instance tends towards the grotesque:

"Your wig fits very well," the Wasp murmured, looking at her with an expression of admiration: "It's the shape of your head as does it. Your jaws ain't well shaped, though—I should think you couldn't bite well?" Alice began with a little scream of laughter, which she turned into a cough as well as she could. At last she managed to say gravely, "I can bite anything I want."

"Not with a mouth as small as that," the Wasp persisted. "If you was a-fighting now—could you get hold of the other one by the back of the neck?"

"I'm afraid not," said Alice.

"Well, that's because your jaws are too short," the Wasp went on: "but the top of your head is nice and round." He took off his own wig as he spoke, and stretched out one claw towards Alice, as if he wished to do the same for her, but she kept out of reach, and would not take the hint. So he went on with his criticisms.

The discovery of a previously unseen work by Carroll is naturally of great significance to scholars and critics. Like the forthcoming Carroll letters (edited by Morton Cohen), "The Wasp in a Wig" will open new discussions of Carroll's life and work. *Time* magazine and the New York *Times* have already heralded the unearthing of "The Wasp in a Wig." Paradoxically, the mystery surrounding the discovery of this episode after a lapse of over one hundred years may turn out to be more interesting than the episode itself.

Notes and References

Chapter One

1. Stuart Collingwood, quoted in Derek Hudson, *Lewis Carroll* (London, 1954), p. 25.

2. Phyllis Greenacre, *Swift and Carroll: A Psychoanalytic Study of Two Lives* (New York, 1955), p. 217.

3. Florence B. Lennon, *Lewis Carroll* (London, 1947), p. 14.

4. *The Annotated Alice: Alice's Adventures in Wonderland and Through the Looking Glass,* ed. Martin Gardner (New York, 1960). p. 308.

5. Lennon, *Lewis Carroll,* p. 22.

6. Quoted in Hudson, *Lewis Carroll,* p. 27.

7. *The Diaries of Lewis Carroll,* ed. Roger Lancelyn Green (2 vols.; New York, 1954), I, 9–10.

8. *Ibid.,* p. 10.

9. *Ibid.,* p. 12.

10. Quoted in Hudson, *Lewis Carroll,* p. 46.

11. *Ibid.,* p. 51.

12. *Ibid.,* p. 57.

13. *Diaries,* I, 50.

14. *Ibid.,* p. 70.

15. *Ibid.,* pp. 77–78.

16. *Ibid.,* p. 78.

17. *Ibid.,* p. 79.

18. *Ibid.,* p. 86.

19. Helmut Gernsheim, *Lewis Carroll, Photographer* (New York, 1949), p. 28.

20. *Diaries,* I, p. 83.

21. *Ibid.,* p. 111.

22. *Ibid.,* pp. 181–82.

23. *Ibid.,* p. 182.

24. *Ibid.,* pp. 230–31.

25. Quoted in Hudson, *Lewis Carroll,* p. 140.

26. *The Athenaeum* (Dec. 16, 1865), p. 844.

27. Quoted in the introduction to *The Annotated Snark,* ed. Martin Gardner (New York, 1962), p. 11.

28. *Aspects of Alice, Lewis Carroll's Dreamchild as seen through the Critics' Looking-Glasses,* ed. Robert Phillips (New York, 1971), p. 94.

29. Quoted in Hudson, *Lewis Carroll,* p. 140.

30. *Ibid.,* p. 140.

31. "Journal of a Tour in Russia in 1867," *The Works of Lewis Carroll,* ed. Roger Lancelyn Green (Feltham, 1965), p. 968.

32. *Ibid.,* p. 974.

33. *Ibid.,* p. 975.

34. *Ibid.,* p. 977.

35. *Ibid.,* p. 983.

36. *Ibid.,* p. 1005.

37. Hudson, *Lewis Carroll,* p. 166.

38. Lennon, *Lewis Carroll,* p. 152.

39. *Diaries,* II, 263.

40. Quoted in Hudson, *Lewis Carroll,* p. 167.

41. *Ibid.,* p. 173.

42. *Diaries,* II, 272.

43. Quoted in Hudson, *Lewis Carroll,* p. 180.

44. *Ibid.,* pp. 270–71.

45. *Ibid.,* pp. 271–72.

46. *Diaries,* II, 501.

47. *Ibid.,* p. 400.

48. *Ibid.,* p. 411.

49. *Ibid.,* p. 445.

50. " 'Alice' on the Stage," *The Works of Lewis Carroll,* ed. Roger Lancelyn Green, p. 237.

51. *Diaries,* II, 469.

52. *The Athenaeum* (Jan. 4, 1890), pp. 11–12.

53. Quoted in Hudson, *Lewis Carroll,* p. 291.

54. *Ibid.,* p. 301.

55. *Diaries,* II, 501.

56. Quoted in Hudson, *Lewis Carroll,* p. 309.

Chapter Two

1. *The Rectory Umbrella and Mischmasch,* with a foreword by Florence Milner (New York, 1971), p. vi.

2. *Ibid.,* p. 11. Subsequent references to this work will be indicated in the text.

3. *Ibid.,* p. 8. Subsequent references to this work will be indicated in the text.

4. *The Oxford History of English Art* (11 vols.; Oxford, 1959), X, 159.

5. *The Rectory Umbrella and Mischmasch,* p. 15. Subsequent references to this work will be indicated in the text.

Chapter Three

1. *The Humorous Verse of Lewis Carroll* (New York, 1960), p. 404. All of the poems in section I are from this book and page numbers will be cited in the text.

2. John Skinner, "Lewis Carroll's Adventures in Wonderland," *American Imago,* 4 (1947), 3–31; rpt. in *Aspects of Alice,* ed. Robert Phillips, p. 299.

3. Derek Hudson, *Lewis Carroll,* p. 188.

4. Alexander L. Taylor, *The White Knight* (Edinburgh, 1952), p. 31.

5. Quoted in Taylor, *The White Knight,* p. 32.

6. Elizabeth Sewell, *The Field of Nonsense* (London, 1952).

7. *Ibid.,* p. 20.

8. *Ibid.,* p. 112.

9. *Ibid.,* p. 113.

10. "Lewis Carroll and T. S. Eliot as Nonsense Poets," *T. S. Eliot,* ed. Neville Braybrooke (New York, 1958), pp. 49–56; rpt. in *Aspects of Alice,* ed. Robert Phillips, p. 119.

11. "Today's 'Wonder-World' Needs Alice, *New York Times Magazine* (July 1, 1962), p. 5; rpt. in *Aspects of Alice,* p. 6.

12. *The Humorous Verse of Lewis Carroll,* pp. 10–11.

13. *Ibid.,* pp. 7–8.

14. *Swift and Carroll: A Psychoanalytic Study of Two Lives,* p. 214.

15. *The Rectory Umbrella and Mischmasch,* pp. 96–103.

16. *The Annotated Alice,* p. 159.

17. *Ibid.,* p. 159.

18. *Ibid.,* p. 158.

19. *The Rectory Umbrella and Mischmasch,* pp. 136–39.

20. *Ibid.,* pp. 143–47.

21. *The Humorous Verse of Lewis Carroll,* pp. 44–46.

22. *The Annotated Alice,* p. 311.

23. All of the poems quoted below are from *The Annotated Alice;* subsequent page references will be cited in the text.

24. "A Burble through the Tulgey Wood," *How Does a Poem Mean?* (Boston, 1959), pp. 678–85; rpt. in *Aspects of Alice,* p. 258.

25. *The Field of Nonsense,* pp. 100–101.

26. "Alice's Journey to the End of Night," *PMLA*, 81 (Oct., 1966). 324.

27. *The Annotated Alice*, p. 140.

28. *Ibid.*, p. 192.

29. *The Field of Nonsense*, p. 118.

30. *Ibid.*, pp. 119–20.

31. *Ibid.*, p. 122.

32. "What is a Boojum? Nonsense and Modernism," *Yale French Studies*, 43 (1969), 145–64; rpt. in *Alice in Wonderland*, ed. Donald J. Gray (New York, 1971), p. 412.

33. *The White Knight*, p. 80.

34. *Ibid.*, pp. 80–81.

35. *The Annotated Alice*, p. 197.

36. *Ibid.*, p. 235.

37. *Ibid.*, p. 237.

38. *The Field of Nonsense*, p. 113.

39. *The Annotated Alice*, p. 333.

40. " 'Alice' on the Stage," *The Works of Lewis Carroll*, ed. Roger Lancelyn Green, pp. 235–36.

41. *The Athenaeum*, 67 (April 8, 1876), 495.

42. " 'Alice' on the Stage," *The Works of Lewis Carroll*, p. 236.

43. The above readings of the poem are cited in *The Annotated Snark*, ed. Martin Gardner, pp. 19–20.

44. *The Enchafed Flood* (New York, 1967), p. 63.

45. *Yale French Studies*, 43 (1969), 145–64; rpt. in *Alice in Wonderland*, ed. Donald J. Gray, pp. 402–18.

46. *Ibid.*, pp. 404–405.

47. *Ibid.*, pp. 412–16.

48. *Ibid.*, p. 417.

49. All of the quotations from the poem are from *The Annotated Snark*; page numbers for subsequent quotations will be cited in the text.

50. *The Annotated Snark*, p. 23.

51. *Swift and Carroll: A Psychoanalytic Study of Two Lives*. pp. 244–45.

52. *The Annotated Snark*, pp. 65–66.

Chapter Four

1. Derek Hudson, *Lewis Carroll*, p. 146.

2. "*Alice in Wonderland* in Perspective," *Aspects of Alice*, ed. Robert Phillips, pp. 89–90.

3. *The Annotated Alice,* ed. Martin Gardner, p. 26; page numbers for subsequent quotations will be cited in the text.

4. *Some Versions of Pastoral* (New York, 1960), pp. 256–57.

5. Florence Becker Lennon, *Lewis Carroll,* p. 123.

6. Martin Gardner, *The Annotated Alice,* p. 30.

7. "The Alice Books and the Metaphors of Victorian Childhood," *Aspects of Alice,* ed. Robert Phillips, p. 102.

8. "Alice's Journey to the End of Night," *PMLA,* 81 (Oct., 1966), 325.

9. *Ibid.,* p. 316.

10. Donald Rackin, "Alice's Journey to the End of Night," pp. 315–16.

11. *Some Versions of Pastoral,* p. 255.

12. *Ibid.,* p. 260.

13. "The Alice Books and the Metaphors of Victorian Childhood," pp. 105–106.

14. Martin Gardner, *The Annotated Alice,* p. 48.

15. *Some Versions of Pastoral,* p. 259.

16. "Lewis Carroll and T. S. Eliot as Nonsense Poets," *Aspects of Alice,* ed. Robert Phillips, p. 124.

17. *Some Versions of Pastoral,* p. 258.

18. "Alice as *Anima*: the Image of Woman in Carroll's Classic," *Aspects of Alice,* p. 386.

19. Donald Rackin's "Alice's Journey to the End of Night," p. 320.

20. *The Field of Nonsense,* p. 113.

21. "The Philosopher's *Alice in Wonderland,*" *The Antioch Review,* 19 (1959), 133–49; rpt. in *Aspects of Alice,* p. 161.

22. "Alice's Journey to the End of Night," p. 321.

23. *Some Versions of Pastoral* (New York, 1960), pp. 263–64.

24. "*Alice in Wonderland* in Perspective," pp. 91–92.

25. *Ibid.,* p. 92.

26. *The Annotated Alice,* p. 124.

27. "Alice's Journey to the End of Night." p. 324.

28. "Lewis Carroll and the Oxford Movement," *Aspects of Alice,* p. 216.

29. Elsie Leach, "*Alice in Wonderland* in Perspective," p. 92.

30. "The Alice Books and the Metaphors of Victorian Childhood," *Aspects of Alice,* p. 111.

31. "The Philosopher's *Alice in Wonderland,*" *Aspects of Alice,* p. 169.

32. *Ibid.,* p. 170.

33. "Logic and Language in *Through the Looking-Glass,*" *ETC,* 18, (1961), 91–100; rpt. in *Aspects of Alice,* p. 269.

34. *The White Knight,* p. 101.

35. Martin Gardner, *The Annotated Alice,* p. 172.

36. Taylor, *The White Knight,* p. 98.

37. Gardner elaborates upon some of these techniques in *The Annotated Alice,* pp. 180–83.

38. *Some Versions of Pastoral,* p. 271.

39. See William Empson, *Some Versions of Pastoral,* for a fuller treatment of the theme of the nineteenth-century child's relationship to nature.

40. *The Annotated Alice,* p. 239.

41. *Some Versions of Pastoral,* p. 277.

42. *Mathematical Recreations of Lewis Carroll: Symbolic Logic and The Game of Logic* (New York, 1958), p. 166.

43. "A Note on Humpty Dumpty," *I for One* (New York, 1921). pp. 191–99; rpt. in *Aspects of Alice,* p. 264.

44. *The Annotated Alice,* p. 296.

45. Judith Bloomingdale, "Alice as *Anima*: the Image of Woman in Carroll's Classic," p. 388.

46. Empson, *Some Versions of Pastoral,* p. 253.

47. "Laughter," in *Comedy,* introd. by Wylie Sypher (New York, 1956), p. 63; page numbers for subsequent quotations will be cited in the text.

Chapter Five

1. "Preface," *Sylvie and Bruno,* in *The Works of Lewis Carroll,* ed. Roger Lancelyn Green, pp. 379, 381.

2. "Preface," *Sylvie and Bruno Concluded,* in *The Works of Lewis Carroll,* ed. Roger Lancelyn Green, p. 539.

3. Quoted in A. L. Taylor, *The White Knight,* p. 179.

4. "Preface," *Sylvie and Bruno Concluded,* p. 539.

5. *Sylvie and Bruno,* in *The Works of Lewis Carroll,* ed. Roger Lancelyn Green, p. 533; quotations from both *Sylvie and Bruno* and *Sylvie and Bruno Concluded* are from the above edition, and subsequent page references will be cited in the text.

6. "C. L. Dodgson: The Poet Logician," *The Shores of Light* (New York, 1952), pp. 540–50; rpt. in *Aspects of Alice,* ed. Robert Phillips p. 202.

7. Florence Becker Lennon, *Lewis Carroll,* p. 220.

8. *Ibid.,* p. 219.

9. *Ibid.,* p. 227.

10. *Ibid.,* p. 220.

11. Derek Hudson, *Lewis Carroll,* p. 287.

12. *Ibid.,* p. 289.

13. "C. L. Dodgson: The Poet Logician," *Aspects of Alice,* ed. Robert Phillips, p. 203.

14. *Ibid.,* p. 202.

15. Hudson, *Lewis Carroll,* p. 287.

16. *Swift and Carroll: A Psychoanalytic Study of Two Lives,* p. 227.

17. *Ibid.,* p. 230.

18. *Ibid.,* p. 211.

19. Hudson, *Lewis Carroll,* p. 289.

Chapter Six

1. Quoted in Florence Becker Lennon, *Lewis Carroll,* p. 166.

2. Elizabeth Sewell, *The Field of Nonsense,* p. 112.

3. *Swift and Carroll: A Psychoanalytic Study of Two Lives,* p. 212.

4. *Ibid.,* p. 240.

5. *Lewis Carroll Photographer,* p. 16.

6. *Ibid.,* p. 79.

7. *Ibid.,* p. 21.

8. *Ibid.*

9. *Ibid.*

10. *Ibid.*

11. *Ibid.,* p. 57.

12. *Ibid.,* p. 58.

13. *Ibid.,* p. 50.

14. *Ibid.,* p. 74.

15. Florence Becker Lennon, *Lewis Carroll,* p. 165.

16. Evelyn Hatch, *A Selection from the Letters of Lewis Carroll to his Child Friends* (London, 1933), p. 3.

17. "The Mathematical manuscripts of Lewis Carroll," *The Princeton University Library Chronicle,* 16 (1954–55), 4–9; rpt. in *Alice in Wonderland,* ed. Donald J. Gray, p. 291.

18. *The Magic of Lewis Carroll,* ed. John Fisher (New York, 1973), p. 8.

19. *The Works of Lewis Carroll,* ed. Roger Lancelyn Green, p. 908.

20. *Ibid.,* pp. 901–902.

21. *Euclid and His Modern Rivals* (New York, 1973), pp. 1–2.

22. *Ibid.,* p. 17.

23. *Ibid.,* p. 54.

24. *Ibid.*, pp. 182–83.

25. "Lewis Carroll as Logician," *Mathematical Gazette*, 16 (1932). 174–78; rpt. in *Alice in Wonderland*, ed. Donald J. Gray (New York. 1971), p. 298.

26. *Mathematical Recreations of Lewis Carroll: Symbolic Logic and The Game of Logic* (New York, 1958), p. 25.

27. *Ibid.*, pp. 164–65.

28. Braithwaite, pp. 301–302.

29. *Mathematical Recreations*, p. 166.

30. *The Works of Lewis Carroll*, pp. 1089, 1090, 1092.

31. *Ibid.*, p. 1099.

32. *Ibid.*, p. 964.

33. *The Idea of a University* (New York, 1947), p. 88.

34. Quoted in Derek Hudson, *Lewis Carroll*, p. 283.

35. *Ibid.*, p. 284.

36. *The Works of Lewis Carroll*, p. 1071.

37. *Ibid.*, p. 1072.

38. *Ibid.*, p. 1072.

39. *Ibid.*, p. 1074.

Chapter Seven

1. *The Magic of Lewis Carroll*, ed. John Fisher, p. 274.

2. "C. L. Dodgson: The Poet Logician," *Aspects of Alice*, ed. Robert Phillips, p. 198.

3. Quoted in *The Annotated Snark*, ed. Martin Gardner, p. 17.

4. "C. L. Dodgson: The Poet Logician," *Aspects of Alice*, p. 202.

5. Quoted in Kathleen Blake, *Play, Games and Sport* (Ithaca and London, 1974), p. 11.

6. "Introduction," *Alice in Wonderland* (New York, 1971), p. xi.

7. Quoted in Derek Hudson, *Lewis Carroll*, p. 303.

8. "Alice as *Anima:* the Image of Woman in Carroll's Classic," *Aspects of Alice*, p. 383.

9. *Finnegans Wake* (New York, 1959), p. 482.

Selected Bibliography

PRIMARY SOURCES

CARROLL, LEWIS. *Alice's Adventures Under Ground, Being a Fac-simile of the Original Ms. Book Afterwards Developed Into "Alice's Adventures in Wonderland."* New York: MacMillan, 1886.
————. *The Annotated Alice: Alice's Adventures in Wonderland and Through the Looking Glass,* ed. Martin Gardner. New York: Clarkson N. Potter, 1960.
————. *The Annotated Snark,* ed. Martin Gardner. New York: Simon and Schuster, 1962.
————. *The Diaries of Lewis Carroll,* ed. Roger Lancelyn Green. 2 vols. New York: Oxford University Press, 1954.
————. *Euclid and His Modern Rivals.* New York: Dover Publications, Inc., 1973.
————. *The Humorous Verse of Lewis Carroll.* New York: Dover Publications, Inc., 1960.
————. *The Magic of Lewis Carroll,* ed. John Fisher, New York: Simon and Schuster, 1973.
————. *Mathematical Recreations of Lewis Carroll: Symbolic Logic and The Game of Logic.* New York: Dover Publications, Inc., 1958.
————.*The Rectory Umbrella and Mischmasch,* with a foreword by Florence Milner. New York: Dover Publications, Inc., 1971.
————. *A Selection from the Letters of Lewis Carroll to his Child Friends,* ed. Evelyn Hatch, London: Macmillan, 1933.
————. *The Unknown Lewis Carroll,* ed. Stuart Dodgson Collingwood. New York: Dover Publications, Inc., 1961.
————. *The Works of Lewis Carroll,* ed. Roger Lancelyn Green. Feltham: Spring Books, 1965.

SECONDARY SOURCES

ANON. "Children's Books," *The Athenaeum* (Dec. 16, 1865), p. 844. A review of *Alice's Adventures in Wonderland.*
————. [Review of *The Hunting of the Snark*], *The Athenaeum,* 67 (April 8, 1876), 495.

—————. [Review of *Sylvie and Bruno*], *The Athenaeum* (Jan. 4, 1890). pp. 11–12.

AUDEN, W. H. "Today's 'Wonder-World' Needs Alice," *New York Times Magazine* (July 1, 1962), p. 5. Reprinted in *Aspects of Alice*, ed. Robert Phillips. Random but perceptive commentary on the two Alice books.

BERGSON, HENRI. "Laughter," in *Comedy*, introd. by Wylie Sypher. New York: Doubleday and Co., 1956. Analyzes the basic principles of humor.

BLAKE, KATHLEEN. *Play, Games and Sport: The Literary Works of Lewis Carroll.* Ithaca and London: Cornell University Press, 1974. Examines Carroll's philosophy of play.

BLOOMINGDALE, JUDITH. "Alice as *Anima*: the Image of Woman in Carroll's Classic," *Aspects of Alice*, ed. Robert Phillips. New York: The Vanguard Press, Inc., 1971. A Jungian study of Alice as Carroll's *anima.*

CIARDI, JOHN. "A Burble Through the Tulgey Wood," *How Does a Poem Mean?* Boston: Houghton, Mifflin, 1959. Reprinted in *Aspects of Alice*, ed. Robert Phillips. Discusses a few of the poems in the Alice books.

COLLINGWOOD, STUART DODGSON. *The Life and Letters of Lewis Carroll.* London: T. Fisher Unwin, 1898. The standard family biography, by Carroll's nephew.

EMPSON, WILLIAM. *Some Versions of Pastoral.* New York: New Directions, 1960. A rambling but brilliant chapter on Alice as "swain" (pp. 241–282).

GERNSHEIM, HELMUT. *Lewis Carroll Photographer.* New York: Chanticleer Press Inc., 1949. A comprehensive study of Carroll's photographic art, with 64 photographic plates.

GORDON, JAN B. "The Alice Books and the Metaphors of Victorian Childhood," *Aspects of Alice*, ed. Robert Phillips. New York: The Vanguard Press, Inc., 1971. Argues that the Alice books are decadent adult literature.

GRAY, DONALD J., ed. *Alice in Wonderland* (a Norton Critical Edition). New York: W. W. Norton & Company, 1971. Reprints the texts of *Alice's Adventures in Wonderland* and *Through the Looking-Glass* based upon those editions Carroll prepared for the press; also includes the 1876 version of *The Hunting of the Snark* and several biographical and critical essays.

GREEN, ROGER LANCELYN, ed. *The Lewis Carroll Handbook.* London: Oxford University Press, 1962. Invaluable for bibliographic and factual details.

GREENACRE, PHYLLIS. *Swift and Carroll: A Psychoanalytic Study of Two Lives.* New York: International Universities Press, 1955. The most intelligent and provocative psychoanalytic study of Carroll to date.

HINZ, JOHN. "Alice Meets the Don," *South Atlantic Quarterly,* 52 (1953), 253–66. Relates the Alice books to *Don Quixote.*

HOLMES, ROGER W. "The Philosopher's *Alice in Wonderland,*" *Antioch Review,* 19 (1959), 133–49. Reprinted in *Aspects of Alice,* ed. Robert Phillips. Discusses the reality of names, identity, and time.

HOLQUIST, MICHAEL. "What is a Boojum? Nonsense and Modernism, *Yale French Studies,* 43 (1969), 145–64. Reprinted in *Alice in Wonderland,* ed. Donald J. Gray. Argues that *The Hunting of the Snark* can only be understood as a closed system of language.

HUDSON, DEREK. *Lewis Carroll.* London: Constable, 1954. The best biography to date.

LEACH, ELSIE. "*Alice in Wonderland* in Perspective," *Aspects of Alice,* ed. Robert Phillips. New York: The Vanguard Press, Inc., 1971. A study of Alice against the background of Victorian children's literature.

LENNON, FLORENCE BECKER. *Lewis Carroll.* London: Cassell & Co. Ltd., 1947. Although slightly disorganized, this book contains much information found in no other biography and contains some excellent literary criticism and psychological insights.

LESLIE, SHANE. "Lewis Carroll and the Oxford Movement," *Aspects of Alice,* ed. Robert Phillips. New York: The Vanguard Press, Inc., 1971. Examines the Alice books as allegories of the Oxford Movement.

NEWMAN, JOHN HENRY. *The Idea of a University.* New York: Longman's, Green and Co., 1947.

The Oxford History of English Art. 11 vols. Oxford: Oxford University Press, 1959.

PHILLIPS, ROBERT. *Aspects of Alice, Lewis Carroll's Dreamchild as seen through the critics' looking-glasses.* New York: The Vanguard Press, Inc., 1971. The largest single collection of critical essays and a useful bibliography of items from 1865–1971.

PITCHER, GEORGE, "Wittgenstein, Nonsense, and Lewis Carroll," *The Massachusetts Review,* 6 (1965), 591–611. Demonstrates that Wittgenstein and Carroll were both professionally concerned with nonsense.

PRIESTLEY, J. B. "A Note on Humpty Dumpty," *I for One.* New York:

Dodd, Mead, 1921. Reprinted in *Aspects of Alice*, ed. Robert Phillips. Argues convincingly that Humpty Dumpty is a satire of the solemn literary pedant.

RACKIN, DONALD, ed. *Alice's Adventures in Wonderland, A Critical Handbook.* Belmont, California: Wadsworth Publishing Company, Inc., 1961. Reproduces the Rosenbach facsimile of *Alice's Adventures under Ground* and the text of *Alice's Adventures in Wonderland* (based upon a number of editions supervised by Carroll); also contains a dozen critical essays and a helpful bibliography.

————. "Alice's Journey to the End of Night," *PMLA*, 81 (October, 1966), 313–26. An existential reading of *Alice's Adventures in Wonderland* in which Alice's experiences represent man's search for meaning in a meaningless world.

SEWELL, ELIZABETH. *The Field of Nonsense.* London: Chatto and Windus, 1952. A brilliant study of the principles of nonsense. based upon logical and linguistic considerations.

————. "Lewis Carroll and T. S. Eliot as Nonsense Poets," in *T. S. Eliot,* ed. Neville Braybrooke. New York: Farrar, Straus, 1958. Reprinted in *Aspects of Alice*, ed. Robert Phillips. Examines the principles of nonsense that are exhibited in the work of both Eliot and Carroll.

SKINNER, JOHN. "Lewis Carroll's Adventures in Wonderland," *American Imago*, 4 (1947), 3–31. Reprinted in *Aspects of Alice*, ed. Robert Phillips. A psychoanalytic approach to Carroll's writings.

SPACKS, PATRICIA MEYER. "Logic and Language in *Through the Looking Glass*," *ETC*, 18 (1961), 91–100. Reprinted in *Aspects of Alice*, ed. Robert Phillips. Argues that language is a theme that underlies virtually all of the episodes in *Through the Looking-Glass.*

TAYLOR, ALEXANDER L. *The White Knight.* London: Oliver and Boyd, 1952. Relates the Alice books to contemporary religious controversies.

WEAVER, WARREN. "The Mathematical Manuscripts of Lewis Carroll," *The Princeton University Library Chronicle*, 16 (1954–55), 4–9. Reprinted in *Alice in Wonderland*, ed. Donald J. Gray. Contends that Carroll's mathematical writings are elementary but often enlivened through whimsy and nonsense.

WILSON, EDMUND. "C. L. Dodgson: The Poet Logician," in *The Shores of Light.* New York: Farrar, Straus, 1952. Reprinted in *Aspects of Alice*, ed. Robert Phillips. A brilliant but brief commentary on Carroll and Carrollian criticism.

Index

(The works of Carroll are listed under his name)

159

DATE DUE

11·21.90			